Japanese Legacy

To Gary,
J. J. Lukes

Timothy J. Lukes
and Gary Y. Okihiro

Farming and Community Life in California's Santa Clara Valley

Japanese Legacy

by Timothy J. Lukes and Gary Y. Okihiro
with a foreword by Norman Y. Mineta, M.C.

Local History Studies Volume 31
California History Center
Cupertino, California

Farming and Community Life in California's Santa Clara Valley

Edited by Jane Goodson Lawes.
Photos edited by Duane Kubo.
Copyright © by California History Center, 1985.
All rights reserved, including the right of
reproduction in any form. Published by the
California History Center, De Anza College,
21250 Stevens Creek Blvd., Cupertino, California,
95014.

10 9 8 7 6 5 4 3 2 1

First Edition

Library of Congress Cataloging-in-Publication Data

Lukes, Timothy J., 1950-
    Japanese Legacy.
    (Local history studies, ISSN 0276-4105 ; v. 31)
    Bibliography; p. 141
    Includes index.
    1. Japanese Americans—California—Santa Clara Valley—History. 2. Japanese American farmers—
    California—Santa Clara Valley— History. 3. Migrant agricultural laborers—California—Santa Clara
    Valley—History. 4. Santa Clara Valley (Calif.)—History. I. Okihiro, Gary Y., 1945-   . II. Lawes,
    Jane Goodson. III. Title. IV. Series. F868.S25L85 1985 979.4'7 85-19478

Local History Studies • Volume 31 • ISSN 0276-4105
ISBN 0-935089-08-X
ISBN 0-935089-09-8 (pbk.)

TO

JAPANESE FARMERS

Whose

Individual Struggles

Gave Substance to

Our Collective History

Japanese Legacy was made possible though a grant
given to the California History Center Foundation
by the California Council for the Humanities,
the state branch of the National Endowment for
the Humanities.

Matching funds were provided by:

Noburo, Eddie, and Albert Ando
Cupertino Nursery and Florist
Tom Takeshi Ezaki
Hitachi America Ltd.
Japanese-American Citizens League, San Jose Chapter
Tom Kawahara
Mayfair Nurseries Inc., Herb and Bill Takeda
Congressman Norman Y. Mineta
The Mitsubishi Bank of California
Mountain View Greenhouses Inc., Oku Family
Nikkei Matsuri Committee
Oyama Brothers Inc., Wright Oyama
Eiichi Sakauye
Y. Uchida and Company Inc.
Austen D. Warburton
Eiko Yamaichi
Jimi Yamaichi
Masaru and Itsuye Yamaichi
Henry and Kikuye Yamate

and the Membership of the
California History Center Foundation

The findings, conclusions, and opinions presented
herein do not necessarily represent the views of
either the California Council for the Humanities,
the National Endowment for the Humanities, or the
California History Center Foundation.

CONTENTS

LIST OF MAPS

LIST OF TABLES

FOREWORD
Norman Y. Mineta, M.C.

Americans of Japanese ancestry, indeed all Americans whose forebears were immigrants, will be grateful to Timothy Lukes and Gary Okihiro for writing this book, *Japanese Legacy.* This book tells the story of the Japanese immigrants who came to the Santa Clara Valley to work in the agricultural sector, and their economic and social struggle to become a part of that community. The story they tell is a microcosm of the struggle of the Americans of Japanese ancestry to become a part of this country.

I am grateful for this book because when one hears Americans tell of the immigrants who built this nation, one is often led to believe that all our forebears came from Europe. When one hears stories about the pioneers going West to shape the land, the Asian immigrant is rarely mentioned. In this book, our story is told. It tells that Americans of Asian ancestry also toiled with the earth and shaped the land.

However, our immigrant history differs from that of the European immigrants'. This book clearly shows how Japanese immigrants made crucial economic contributions to the valley, but were discriminated against by elements of the white community who endeavored to exclude them from the wider community and to prevent a permanent Japanese American community from developing.

As I read through the manuscript that was to become this book, I saw in my mind's eye the story of my father. He came from a farming family in Japan. When my father was fourteen, my grandfather, wanting his son to study American farming

techniques, sent my father to his uncle in Salinas, California. My great-uncle was working for the Spreckels Sugar Company growing sugar beets. My father sailed across the Pacific alone and, not knowing a word of English, disembarked from the boat in Seattle. He worked his way in lumber camps and farms down to Salinas. When he reached Salinas, he joined Spreckels Sugar Company and after eight years there, the company sent him to manage one of its San Jose farming operations. My father gave up farming after hospitalization from a serious case of influenza, and eventually began a small insurance agency which I still own and operate.

I tell this story, not because my parents were so unusual, but because they were so typical of the courage and determination that drives all immigrants. More than anything else, my parents, and the Japanese immigrants whose story is told in this book, were people of strength, determination, and endurance. They would not have survived if they were not.

In 1942, the U.S. government caved in to anti-Japanese sentiment and instituted a racist policy nationwide to intern Americans of Japanese ancestry. After having struggled so hard to build their lives, everything seemed to sift through their fingers like sand. My family too was interned. It is heartbreaking to hear the recounting of the financial and emotional toll the internment had on those who were interned. It is painful to hear the immigrants explain the sorrow they felt in having lost all they had gained through backbreaking work, only to face the prospect of starting over as if they had arrived in the country the day before.

I am proud of the achievements of the Japanese immigrants as well as the achievements of their descendants. Many of the descendants who now reside or work in Santa Clara Valley are successful in areas other than agriculture, such as business, education, and science. Yet, it behooves the present generation of Americans of Japanese ancestry to know their past, so that they can understand where they stand today. *Japanese Legacy* is a big step to a better understanding of who we are and how we began in this country.

ACKNOWLEDGMENTS

Japanese Legacy owes much to many individuals and organizations. We acknowledge that debt with gratitude.

The idea for the book originated in the spring of 1983 when co-author Okihiro presented a paper on Japanese losses in California agriculture during World War II at a conference in Salt Lake City. Okihiro was fortunate to have as his traveling companion Eiichi Sakauye — local farmer, longtime resident of the Santa Clara Valley, and historian of the San Jose Japanese American community. Several hours were spent in conversation about Okihiro's paper and especially on Sakauye's experiences in the valley, the impact of World War II on the farming community, and the return of Japanese Americans to the valley. Sakauye encouraged Okihiro to undertake a regional study of Japanese farmers in the Santa Clara Valley to test his ideas put forward in his paper on Japanese farmers in California as a whole. Thus was born the Japanese Farmers in the Santa Clara Valley Project.

Co-author Lukes joined the project bringing to it his long interest in civil rights and expertise in local government and California politics. In July of 1983, San Jose Mayor Thomas McEnery appointed Lukes to the San Jose Commission on the Internment of Local Japanese Americans. The commission was established to study the impact of World War II on the local Japanese American community, and to make recommendations for appropriate redress. Through Lukes, the work of the commission and our Japanese farming project were coordinated and intimately tied.

Duane Kubo, photographer and filmmaker, developed a photo archive for the project and a videotape on the Japanese farming experience in the valley. His visual documentation greatly enhances the value of the project's collection of historical materials and of this book. Historian Sucheng Chan of the University of California, Santa Cruz, generously offered her large and detailed collection of materials on Asian American agricultural history, and pointed us to archives she herself had meticulously searched. We are grateful for her advice and assistance. Finally, we acknowledge the kind help of Professor David W. Eakins of San Jose State University, a specialist on San Jose politics and history.

Various community organizations in the county lent their support, including the San Jose branch of the Japanese American Citizens League, the Nihonmachi Outreach Committee, the Peninsula Redress Committee, the San Jose Commission on the Internment of Local Japanese Americans, and the Santa Clara County Historical Heritage Commission. The San Jose Commission on the Internment of Local Japanese Americans has been instrumental in disseminating portions of our research findings in its final report and curriculum package designed for implementation in Santa Clara County schools. We acknowledge and are grateful for the endorsements of all of these community organizations and for their valued assistance.

But above all, Japanese farmers, the principals of this book, were extremely generous, kind, and helpful. We were strangers, and they welcomed us into their homes and lives. Their contribution to this story is of course immeasurable. We trust that this chronicle of their collective experience will help memorialize their individual struggles and our common debt. We affirm our gratitude to the following Santa Clara Valley farmers: Masuo Akizuki, Yoshio Ando, Harry Araki, Tom Ezaki, John Hayakawa, Kaoru Inouye, Katsusaburo Kawahara, Satoru Kawashima, Henry Kurasaki, Shigio Masunaga, Phil Matsumura, Sue Matsumura, Kazuto Nakamura, Hisao Omori, Eiichi Sakauye, Shoji Takeda, and Tad Tomita.

Seonaid McArthur, director of the California History Center, encouraged us from the start. It was she who first urged us to expand our information into a book. We were inspired in part by the Center's exhibition held in the spring of 1983, "The Japanese Legacy: 1860-1983," which focused on the local Japanese American community. Students at the University of Santa Clara assisted in the frequently tedious and often little appreciated research work. They combed various archives in the Bay Area, read through six decades of the *San Jose Mercury* newspaper, and searched through deeds and court records. Their labor is herewith recognized and their names recorded: Lorraine Abrahamsohn, Marimo Berk, Mildred Bordessa, Sara Burdan, Colleen Crowley, Michael Diepenbrock, David Drummond, Karine Enderle, Lisa Ferdinandsen, Thomas Huckaby, Kathy Klein, Patricia Lai, Nelson Lee, Susan Mahaney, Patrick Mangan, Peter Norrie, Laura Okane, Mayo Ryan, Gerald Sarmento, David Thornley, Jennifer Twitchell, William Wheatley, Betty Young, and Sylvia Zanello.

The project was funded by grants from the American Association for State and Local History, the California Council for the Humanities and the National Endowment for the Humanities, the California History Center, the Sourisseau Academy of San Jose State University, and Dean Joseph L. Subbiondo, College of Arts and Sciences, University of Santa Clara.

Despite our heavy reliance on the individuals and organizations mentioned earlier, any errors of fact and interpretation are, of course, ours. Although both authors contributed something to the overall book, Lukes wrote Chapters 2 and 4 and developed the analysis which linked more sophisticated forms of exploitation to the phase of Japanese agricultural involvement, and Okihiro wrote Chapters 1, 3, 5, 6, 7, and the section entitled "The Anti-Japanese Movement and Public Opinion" in Chapter 4.

CHAPTER 1
INTRODUCTION:
IN STRUGGLE

The central theme of Asian American history is struggle. This book chronicles the struggles of Japanese farmers in California's Santa Clara Valley from around 1895, when they first arrived, to the World War II era. The story, however, is wider than the focus of our book — the Japanese farmers — or the delimited region and time frame. Precedents were established in the valley by Chinese migrants and by the wider social relations that provided the context within which the struggles of Japanese farmers were waged. Further, this story provides a window into the broader past of the experience of Japanese in America as a whole. This study of the Japanese legacy, then, reveals Japanese farmers in struggle.

We undertook this project knowing that very little had been written about Japanese Americans in the Santa Clara Valley, and about Japanese farmers as a whole. Although we made a thorough search of libraries, archives, newspapers, and county land and court records, we expected to find only scattered and peripheral evidence. And we were right. The available data were slim and reflected an outsider's view of the Japanese farming community in the valley. Our aim was to establish Japanese farmers as major figures in the valley's landscape and to portray them as active participants in the making of history. This required seeking out the historical actors themselves, the Japanese farmers, to hear their stories in their own words.

The major portion of this book, accordingly, is based on the recollections of Japanese farmers in the valley. However, while family histories provide the basis upon which this account is based, *Japanese Legacy* is not an assemblage of individual reminiscences. Rather, it offers an interpretation of history. Therefore, it is important that we make explicit the perspectives we have brought to bear on the historical evidence. The following sections briefly summarize those concepts and describe each of the chapters in this book. The major theme of the book is struggle. Struggle, the core and unifying thread of Japanese American history, is revealed in the ideas of inclusion and exclusion, oppression and resistance.

Inclusion and American History

America has been called a nation of immigrants. The saga is a familiar one. Immigrants, displaced by political and religious persecution or by economic hardship, arrive in America where they find equality, religious freedom, and economic opportunities. After an initial period of trial, they achieve success through toil and effort, and are assimilated into the mainstream, adding aspects of their ethnic culture to the great melting pot. In that way, American history is depicted primarily as the process by which immigrants were included in, and contributed to, American society.

Japanese Americans have been similarly viewed. In recent years, the stereotype of the "model minority" has been widely publicized and accepted, and Japanese Americans have been held up as models for emulation. Sociologist William Petersen, in his book titled, *Japanese Americans: Oppression and*

Success, wrote:

> . . .the Japanese case constitutes the outstanding exception to the generalization that past oppression blocks present progress. By almost any criterion of good citizenship that we choose, not only are Japanese Americans better than any other segment of American society, including native whites of native parents, but they have realized this remarkable progress by their own almost unaided effort.[1]

Taking up that theme, others have declared that Japanese Americans have even "outwhited the whites."[2]

Exclusion and American Minority History

An understanding of the history of minorities in America, however, contradicts the notion of inclusion. For example, there was little room for Native Americans on the expanding American frontier. They were, in fact, expelled and excluded through wars of conquest and extermination. Africans were forcibly removed from their homelands, transported across the Atlantic under sub-human conditions, and the survivors were held in bondage in the "peculiar institution." Through conquest Mexicans in the Southwest and California became a part of the United States fulfilling America's "Manifest Destiny." Accordingly, the ways in which those minority groups became Americans belie the "nation of immigrants" tradition.

But what about Asian Americans? Did they not emigrate for the same reasons that Europeans came to America? Were they not seeking better opportunities for themselves and their children? This book maintains that Japanese Americans became incorporated in American society through American imperialism, a stage of capitalism. At first, they were perceived by the dominant class as temporary residents — migrant laborers who would eventually return to Japan. Later, when it became clear that Japanese Americans had established permanent communities in America, their dependency was sought and perpetuated. This book shows that the history of Japanese Americans, like those of America's other minorities, was one of exclusion, not inclusion.

Oppression and Resistance

If the principal theme of Asian American history is struggle, then the struggle was between oppression and resistance. For our purposes, oppression is defined as the social forces that sought to control and exploit individuals or groups, specifically the Japanese. Manifestations of oppression included restrictive immigration, denial of naturalization, controls over reproduction, task segregation, differential wages and rents, mass removal and confinement, cultural modification, and renunciation of citizenship and repatriation. These were exhibited at different stages in the history of the Japanese in America and collectively they form the anti-Japanese movement.

On the other hand, we define resistance as the process whereby the Japanese sought their own self-determination. Resistance was the means by which Japanese Americans sought to frustrate the aims of the anti-Japanese movement. At times, the struggle was engaged at the most basic level of one individual denying the essential humanity of the other; the assertion of one's human dignity, in this instance, was an expression of resistance. The denigration of Japanese culture, for example, was met by cultural persistence and transmission through the Japanese language schools, the ethnic churches, and festivals and cultural entertainment. Labor exploitation resulted in strikes and the threat of strikes by Japanese workers. Other devices employed in the drive for economic self-sufficiency included various strategies for maximizing labor and land, ways devised to escape the restrictive provisions of the alien land laws, and the formation of farm cooperatives. In fact, the very survival of the Japanese community in the valley testifies to the tenacity and efficacy of the Japanese Americans' resistance against oppression.

The struggle between oppression and resistance was dynamic, never static. Thus we view the history of Japanese farmers in the valley as a continuous process of conflicts and changes, interacting and mutually consequential. At the same time, the dominant class determined the latitudes of the struggle and mapped out the terrain of oppression. We begin, accordingly, with a broad survey of the historical context that preceded the entrance of Japanese farmers into the Santa Clara Valley.

Paternalists and Progressives

Just four decades before the arrival of Japanese migrants, the valley was a semi-feudal Mexican frontier, of priests and missions, settlers and ranchos, and Indians exploited for their labor. The Americans transformed the valley into fields and orchards mined for maximum profits. Families like the Murphys dominated the economic and political life of the valley during the 1850s, creating a landed aristocracy and instituting a system of paternalism. During the following decade, however, newcomers representing mercantile and industrial interests began to dismantle the structure erected by the paternalists. These "pre-progressives," exemplified in the person of J.J. Owen, brought industrial capital to the valley during the second half of the nineteenth century, and ushered in the orchard phase and the transition from grains to fruits.

Much of the labor during this period was supplied by Chinese migrants. The Chinese helped to construct the railroad between San Jose and San Francisco, cleared chapparral lands for firewood and agriculture, and pioneered berry farms in the vicinity of Alviso. Their labor was crucial in the economic changeover from grains to orchards. The Chinese migrants' labor was recognized and defended by the pre-progressives as critical to the success of the new fruit industry. The old guard, on the other hand, fanned the flames of anti-Chinese hatred and attacked Owen as "Chinese-loving" and un-American. The anti-Chinese movement in the valley was vehement and directed, wildly exclusionist, and manipulated for political ends. It was within this setting that Japanese farmers arrived in the valley.

Japanese Migrant Labor

Japanese farmers differed from their white

predecessors in the valley. They were not settlers, land speculators, or mercantile capitalists. Like their Chinese precursors, they were migrants in search of work and were tolerated only insofar as they provided useful labor. This concept of migrant labor contradicts the "nation of immigrants" analogy, and helps us to understand the early Japanese farming community in the valley and the nature of the struggle between oppression and resistance.

Properly viewed, Asian American history does not begin with Asian immigration; instead, it commences with Americans going to Asia. In 1784, long before Asians arrived in America, the *Empress of China* set sail from New York harbor with a cargo of ginseng. This voyage inaugurated America's involvement in the China trade. Merchant capital profited from the trade involving furs from the American Northwest, sandalwood from the Hawaiian Kingdom, and products from China. Follow ing the abolition of the African slave trade in the nineteenth century, Yankee clippers carried human cargo — Chinese "coolies" who were destined for the plantations and mines of the Americas. The "opening" of Japan in 1854 and the annexation of Hawaii in 1898 and the Philippines in 1899 were further evidence of America's expanding commercial and strategic interests in the Pacific.

The movement of Asian workers to Hawaii and the West Coast took place under the umbrella of American imperialism. Accordingly, their migration can be viewed as simply another kind of commodity in America's Pacific trade. Plantation managers in Hawaii saw Asian laborers in that way. In 1890, C. McLennan, manager of the Laupahoehoe Plantation, wrote to his factor in Honolulu for bonemeal,

canvas, "Japanese laborers," macaroni, and a "Chinaman."[3] However, Asian workers were more than items of exchange; they were units of labor that in turn were used in the production of capital. That latter characteristic of the profitability of Asian workers is embodied in the concept of migrant labor.

Generally, migrant labor is the movement of laborers from areas of low capital concentration to areas of high capital concentration. The idea derives from the notion of the world as an interlocking network of capital and labor, called the world-system. Within that system are areas of development, called the core, and areas of underdevelopment, called the periphery. Thus, since American imperialism in the Pacific was designed to secure markets and sources of raw materials, commodities, and cheap labor, Asian migrants can properly be viewed as migrant laborers.

The early history of the valley's Japanese farming community, from around 1895 to 1907, bore many characteristics typical of migrant labor. For example, the arrival of Japanese workers coincided with the departure of Chinese workers who were forming labor monopolies in the orchards and fields and were becoming intractable. Japanese migrants were overwhelmingly male and formed a "bachelor society" in Nihonmachi (Japan-town), with its accompanying features of transience, gambling, drinking, and prostitution. Nihonmachi in turn was segregated from the rest of the community and served as a pool of cheap labor for the surrounding orchards. Other features of economic life included task segregation and discriminatory wages. These mechanisms of oppression, maintained through the system of migrant labor, were the daily realities of Japanese migrants.

There was, however, Japanese resistance to the various forms of control and exploitation. Japanese women, for instance, divorced or ran away from oppressive husbands, and Japanese laborers pursued redress against racist attacks through the courts. Strikes and the threat of strikes by Japanese workers resulted in higher wages, and partnerships and collectives enabled the movement from migrant labor to farm tenancy. Before the end of the period of migrant labor, clusters of Japanese farming communities were already growing in Alviso and Agnew. These were genuine communities in contrast to the Nihonmachi bachelor society and denoted permanence in the valley. Their existence posed a challenge to the dominant class and required a different strategy of oppression. The Japanese resistance was met by progressive politics and by the anti-Japanese movement in the valley.

Progressives and the Anti-Japanese Movement

Progressive politics during the orchard phase was more sophisticated than in the preceding paternal and pre-progressive phase. The progressives, although decidedly capitalists, allied themselves with the white labor establishment, but not with the radical cannery and field workers unions. This alliance revealed the true intention of capital in appealing to white workers on the basis of race, and thus dividing the working class. The anti-Japanese movement, accordingly, was framed by the progressives in terms of cultural differences and the inability of the Japanese to assimilate. The unerring

message of the progressives was white supremacy and community homogeneity.

At the same time, capital profited from Japanese labor. The apparent contradiction posed a problem for the dominant class — how to divide the working class (through the anti-Japanese movement) and yet maintain the benefits derived from Japanese labor. The problem was in large part solved by the progressives denouncing the Japanese migrants while not effecting their actual exclusion. For example, although California Senator James D. Phelan was a virulent anti-Asianist, he owned land in the valley on which Japanese farmers share-cropped. And, although the alien land laws were ostensibly designed to drive the Japanese out of agriculture, they were not enforced in the Santa Clara Valley. These strategies by the dominant class clearly served its own interests by both retarding working class consciousness and preserving its profitable relationship with Japanese labor. That, in turn, marked a new stage in the struggle between oppression and resistance, that of dependency.

Japanese Dependency

While migrant labor represents a temporary presence, dependency presumes permanence. The transition here was from "bachelor societies" to settled communities. The period of Japanese dependency, from 1907 to 1942, was characterized by both a rooting in and a rooting out; the embryonic development of a distinctly Japanese American community and the deliberate under-development of that community. The years saw the retrogressive tightening of the alien land laws, the end of the picture-bride system, the Ozawa decision that confirmed the status of Japanese as "aliens ineligible for citizenship," and the 1924 Exclusion Act.

Dependency was the second phase of the struggle. Its characteristics included residential segregation and concentration, economic constraints and exploitation, political powerlessness, and cultural modification. Those features were exhibited in the ethnic ghetto, San Jose's Nihonmachi, and in the Japanese farming clusters scattered throughout the valley floor. Both the location and borders of those communities were permitted and defined by the valley's dominant class, not by their residents. Economic dependency was achieved through public opinion and the alien land laws that enforced task segregation and restricted full participation in the advance of capitalism. As a result, the pattern of farm tenancy included instability and frequent relocation, unconventional tenures leading to further exploitation, and a racial rent premium paid by Japanese farmers. White supremacy was achieved through Japanese underdevelopment.

Resistance during the period of dependency included various strategies to maximize household labor, ingenious uses of land through intensive farming and crop selection and rotation, and the formation of farm corporations to escape the provisions of the alien land law. Japanese farmers shared farm implements, wells, and even laborers; established buying and marketing cooperatives; and sought to regulate prices through planned production. They experimented with new crops such as celery, and modified and invented farm equipment to meet their special needs. They also built Japanese language schools in all of the farming clusters and in Nihonmachi to preserve and transmit Japanese culture, and observed traditional festivals such as Japanese New Year and *obon* to reinforce ethnic and community solidarity.

Despite their dependency, Japanese farmers had resisted and were on the verge of what might have been another transition in the struggle between oppression and resistance. But World War II intervened and presented the dominant class with a "timely opportunity" to repel this new challenge.

Migrant Laborers Once Again

Following December 7, 1941, exclusionists urged the "final solution" to the "Japanese problem." On the national level, Congressman John Rankin of Mississippi declared that he was "for catching every Japanese in America, Alaska, and Hawaii now and putting them in concentration camps and shipping them back to Asia as soon as possible."[4] Expressing that same sentiment, a "leading official" of the Grower-Shipper Vegetable Association wrote to Congressman John Z. Anderson, representing south Santa Clara County, on May 12, 1942:

What can you suggest that I do and thousands of Californians be led to do, that may make it possible to get rid of all Japs, sending them back to Japan either before or after the war is won. I am convinced that if it is not done or at least the action completed before the war is over, it will be impossible to get rid of them. . . . the Japanese cannot be assimilated as the white race [and] we must do everything we can to stop them now as we have a golden opportunity now and may never have it again.[5]

The "golden opportunity" was not missed by those who profited from the dispossession of Japanese farms during the war, nor by the city councils of Morgan Hill and San Jose and the county board of supervisors, all of which passed exclusionist resolutions against the return of the Japanese.

The struggle, raised to a new level by the war, culminated with the expulsion of all Japanese from the valley at the end of May 1942. Despite the harsh rhetoric of exclusionism, there was an underlying consistency in the treatment of Japanese farmers by the dominant class. In the spring of 1942 with removal imminent, they urged a delay in the eviction of Japanese farmers to enable the Japanese to plant their crops. In the summer of 1945, the returning Japanese farmers were welcomed as laborers in saving the year's harvest. In both instances, Japanese farmers were instruments in advancing the interests of capital.

For the Japanese farming community, however, the effects of the war were devastating. Most of the gains made by Japanese farmers in moving toward farm tenancy and ownership were negated by the war. Upon returning to the valley, many had to begin all over again as migrant laborers in the fields and orchards that they once owned or rented. Their return to migrant labor brings full circle our history of Japanese farmers in the Santa Clara Valley, and provides an appropriate ending to this book.

Footnotes

[1] William Petersen, *Japanese Americans: Oppression and Success,* Random House, Inc.: New York, 1971, 4.

[2] "Success Story: Outwhiting the Whites," *Newsweek,* June 21, 1971, 24-25.

[3] Cited in Ronald Takaki, *Pau Hana: Plantation Life and Labor in Hawaii, 1835-1920,* University of Hawaii Press: Honolulu, 1983, 23.

[4] *Congressional Record,* 77th Congress, 2d Session, February 19, 1942, 1419-20.

[5] Quoted in Morton Grodzins, *Americans Betrayed: Politics and the Japanese Evacuation,* University of Chicago Press: Chicago, 1949, 20.

Kiku
CHRYSANTHEMUM

CHAPTER 2
PATERNALISTS AND PRE-PROGRESSIVES, 1849-1899

Japanese immigrants to the Santa Clara Valley were not drawn into a vacuum; rather, historical precedent prepared the social and economic latitudes within which they were to exist. In order to understand the experience of Japanese immigrants in the valley, an "applied" examination of the political and economic history of the valley is essential, especially since such studies have not been forthcoming. What the examination reveals is the interconnectedness between Chinese and Japanese laborers, and the ever-growing sophistication of the means of exploitation (oppression) developed by the community power structure.

The Early American Phase

The early American phase of political and economic development in the valley was ushered in by the California Gold Rush of 1849. In just a few years, and due mostly to enterprises linked at least indirectly to John Sutter's find, the political economy of the valley was transformed from a semifeudal Mexican frontier to an American bastion of Jacksonian (albeit Roman Catholic) ruggedness and agricultural speculation.

Prior to the discovery of gold, only a few Americans had settled in the area of the San Jose pueblo. It was no accident that many of them were poor and of the Catholic faith. Inspired by their priests' stories of Spanish and Mexican missionaries, the new settlers were drawn to a place for which they felt at least a modicum of attachment, and where they hoped they could overcome what

was in most cases economic destitution. In 1844, members of the Martin Murphy family (Irish and Catholic) came overland to California and took advantage of the vast, cheap land parcels by purchasing the Rancho Oja de Agua de la Coste from the Mexican grantees. The new owners were content to graze cattle and maintain subsistence gardens like their Californio neighbors.

The discovery of gold upset this pattern of slow assimilation and instigated a new pattern that ordinarily would have taken much longer to occur. Within days of the loosening of John Marshall's tongue in a Mission San Jose cantina, virtually every male member of the community migrated to the mountains. The Murphys were among the most fortunate and most ingenious — they, like Sheriff Henry Bee, recruited local Indians and exploited their labor for a pittance of what they produced. Martin Murphy, Jr., decided to use some of his newfound wealth to purchase a tract of land that covered most of Sunnyvale. In fact, most of those who were to rise to prominence in the early American period of the valley, including Benjamin Cory, Thomas Fallon, James Reed, and Samuel and Thomas Rea, had the advantages of early settlement and knowledge of the area, combined with gold fortunes made in the mine fields, which enabled them to get a head start in the ensuing transition.

It did not take long for families like the Murphys to realize that they could enhance their income not only by joining the miners, but also by feeding them. A wheat and barley crop, harvested in 1851 in what is now Alameda County,[1] shattered the growing misconception that northern California was fit only for grazing. Soon after, the American landowners in the Santa Clara Valley discovered that, indeed, the treeless "Yolo loam" soil of the northern center of their valley was among the finest in the country for producing grains. (The present center of the area is the town of Santa Clara — between the adobe clays that surround the bay to the north and east, and the more gravelly soil approaching the Santa Cruz mountains on the west.) E.J. Wickson reports that during the 1850s, before it became depleted due to virtually no management practices whatsoever, a particular field in the Santa Clara township produced five barley crops after a single sowing — with the average yield of the last crop at forty-three bushels per acre.[2] In fact, most crops in this era were of the "volunteer grain" variety — grown from seed left on the ground after the last harvesting.

Of course, it was no coincidence that the agricultural potential of the valley was rediscovered in the 1850s. The miners were paying from twenty to fifty dollars per barrel for Chilean flour,[3] and local growers were finding that they could gain substantial profits by selling at much lower prices, and still have time for their claims. In fact, it is clear that the development of intensive agriculture in the Santa Clara Valley was looked upon by the participants in much the same way as they looked upon their mining interests — as a speculative venture with the potential for quick profit. The fact that farmers could brag of five successive barley crops without even plowing the field illustrates the attitude held by the agriculturists toward their land. Because farming was more of an investment than a way of life, the stage of farm self-sufficiency was virtually absent in the development of the valley; crop diversity was eclipsed by large parcels of investment crops. And, of course, that this was at all possible was due to the boom of the gold rush combined with the vast acreages kept intact by the land grant system of the Mexican era.

A Quick Transition

Despite the passage of the Gwin Bill in 1851, the transfer of land from the valley's Spanish-surnamed inhabitants to the incoming Americans continued rapidly. The Gwin Bill created the U.S. Land Commission, which was to carry out the agreement made in the Treaty of Guadalupe Hidalgo that preserved land titles held prior to Americanization. What the Californios came to realize, though, was that they could not withstand the lengthy period of litigation required to retain their titles; their capital was being drained, they were becoming increasingly isolated and alienated in the land they had occupied for many years, they were not as adept at the invaders' legal system, and they did not have the facilities to fight off the multitude of squatters that encroached upon their land. As a result, the lawyers (some of the best in the country could not avoid coming) got rich, and by the middle of the 1860s the number of Spanish surnames in a list of 172 county residents with incomes over $2,800 had dwindled to 12.[4]

The result of this pattern of acquisition was a conflict that was to have lasting implications not only on the economy, but on the politics of the valley. For as the gold fields began to yield a dwindling harvest in the 1860s, settlers began arriving in San Jose in hopes of practicing what had been their original vocation. Rather than finding cheap and available parcels of farmland, they were disappointed to find the land already controlled by a few now prominent families. Sheriff John Murphy's defense of the Chabolla family (one of the few Californio families that tried to retain their land) against a band of angry American squatters has often been referred to as a heroic and selfless defense of justice. But it is clear that in this "Settlers War of 1861," the sheriff was defending not only the rights of the embattled Chabollas, but also the rights of his own family to retain their land under the unpopular treaties and statutes.

The newcomers were able to make some progress, however. To overcome the large land-owners' reticence to sell off mere fractions of their land, late arrivals to the valley who had saved money through sharecropping or as laborers, were combining to form "homestead associations," whereby resources could be pooled and larger tracts purchased and then divided.[5] The smaller operators also had their successes in the new state legislature: in the mid-1860s, bills were passed that placed the burden of enclosure on the livestock rancher rather than the dirt farmer.[6] Combined with a serious drought in 1864,[7] the new laws promoted the sale of a number of the large tracts, and thus there was some diminution of the dominance of the first families.

Landed Aristocracy

Despite the pressure of the land reformers and a budding mercantile class for more "progressive" leadership, the first phase of American settlement in the valley was dominated economically and politically by the large landholders and their proxies. The community leaders had, for the most part, begun their lives in poverty, ignorance, and religious discrimination; but now, suddenly, individuals with names like McGeoghegan, McLaughlin, and Murphy along with Heinrich Alfred Krieser (who under the name Henry Miller came to dominate the cattle industry in the state and much of the southern end of the Santa Clara Valley), Flickinger, Pellier, and Schallenberger had been thrust into positions of economic and political leadership they had not dreamed of a few years earlier.

It was natural, then, and indeed unavoidable, that these first community elites would adopt a style that was decidedly Jacksonian, charismatic, and ethnic. The Murphys were revered by the Catholics and lower-status immigrants in the valley, who could see no advantage in attaching themselves to representatives of the new entrepreneureal middle class (which, ironically, was being drawn to the area by the wealth produced by the large land-holding interests). Capitalizing on their pioneer and ethnic backgrounds, Martin Murphy and his sons, Bernard and James, came to resemble, in the words of Kevin Starr, "ancient Irish Kings."[8] In contrast to the cries for legal-rational procedures coming from the new middle class, the Murphys maintained a strong paternal system, which as late as 1880 attracted many Republicans to the Democratic and Workingmen's Party mayoral candidacy of Bernard Murphy. More like subjects than constituents, they wanted "to show their gratitude."[9]

The Coming of the Chinese

The Chinese, through blatant harassment and discriminatory taxes,[10] were being driven out of California's mining counties. Since San Jose was a terminus for overland traffic, it was no surprise that San Jose was among the first towns to support a Chinese community that was not devoted to mining. Indeed, it was the first American town to use Chinese labor in the construction of a railway (the San Jose–San Francisco Railway) as the new Chinese residents were just about the only people who were willing to do that work for less than one dollar a day.[11] Driven to conditions and wages ever lower by increasing forms of discrimination, the Chinese were an economic windfall to the valley, and became essential to its growth.

As the Chinese community in the valley grew, its place in the work force diversified. The railroad continued to support Chinese laborers, but now as providers of firewood for the boilers. The chapparral lands in the western foothills were being cleared for vineyards, and the manzanita stumps proved excellent fuel for the steam engines. Local farmers found they could sell the wood for more than they needed to pay the Chinese to harvest it. Soon, the Chinese were clearing land not only for agriculture, but for the developing roadway system.

The Chinese also developed pathbreaking berry farms on the alluvial clays of Alviso (later taken over by the Japanese settlers), on land previously thought to be inhospitable to any crop. Otherwise, though, the Chinese were completely unable to break the ownership patterns in the valley, which were by now well-established. In the delta lands along the Sacramento river, where they were able to take mostly unused land and turn it into profitable rice production, some Chinese farmers were able to move from being tenant farmers to owners.[12] In the more agriculturally developed counties such as Santa Clara County, however, the Chinese remained in the tenuous positions of sharecroppers or farm laborers.[13] In the Santa Clara Valley that meant growing vegetable crops for the large landowners who were mainly interested in their investment crops. Virtually all responsibility for garden crops was taken over by the new immigrants in the late 1860s; they were allowed to lease small plots of the large landowners' land and to peddle fruits and vegetables door to door.[14]

Through the 1870s and 1880s, however, the nature of the labor being asked of the Chinese began to change. More and more orchards were being planted by smaller operators who found that orchard crops did not demand the economy of scale found in the grain and livestock concerns. What the orchards demanded, though, was a good deal of intensive labor, and the one or two farmhands of the large ranches were being replaced by crews of laborers who were needed to cultivate and harvest in the embryonic orchards. The canners, too, whose primitive methods demanded extensive hard labor of a repetitive and noxious variety, found that the Chinese were admirable workers, especially as "tinners."[15]

The movement toward orchards and the surrounding canning and peripheral industries brought with it a pre-progressive type of politics that threatened the dominance of the old guard. The Chinese residents of the valley became the unfortunate victims of the political squabble that ensued between the old landed interests and newcomers who were interested in opening up the valley to "progress." In short, while the Chinese were an economic blessing to the large landholders who continued to grow grain and raise cattle, they were still expendable just as they were to the working class Irish and other white ethnics who continued to support the owners.

On the other hand, the new progressives saw Asian labor as crucial to the success of the new fruit industry and the expansion of the valley's economy, and thus they developed an attitude of detached tolerance. The long-established alliance of the old guard and the white ethnic working class in the valley, which was based on the issue of Chinese exclusion, was thus strenthened and the pro-gressives found their attitudes labeled as anti-American and Chinese-loving. As the pressure from the progressive forces increased, the Chinese were no longer employed as laborers, but as the "indispensible enemy" against which the working and owning classes could unite.

The Pre-Progressives

The wealth created by the large farming operations attracted — indeed, necessitated — an influx of constituents that hardly reflected the characteristics of the old guard. To protect, enhance, and exchange the wealth being generated by the grain and livestock industries, San Jose experienced the immigration of a commercial and professional class whose ethnic and educational qualifications differentiated them from their predecessors. For the most part, they were middle class and highly educated, and well aware of the financial opportunities available from orchard crops — opportunities they felt were being hoarded and

hindered by the established regime. Many of them came to prominence first through their efforts to organize fruit growers' cooperatives in the valley.

Archetypical of the new class was J.J. Owen. Having acquired the *San Jose Mercury* in 1861, the former schoolteacher became the champion of progress for the Santa Clara Valley. His argument was that under the old guard, land prices had remained too high to attract new blood to the area, that city services were too poor to attract businesses, and that city politics involved so much cronyism that good ideas and good people, mostly those like himself, were being neglected.[16]

Owen and his pre-progressive colleagues, however, displayed a debilitating naivete that their successors would not. For instance, Owen and virtually all the developing mercantile interests unreservedly lauded the coming of the railroad to San Jose, believing that the link to San Francisco would bring the culture, innovation, and economic spark that the valley needed. He did not anticipate that the Central Pacific was quite receptive to dealing with the paternalistic form of politics and patronage that both it and the old guard of the valley practiced. Until these pre-progressives realized that the railroad was not inherently sympathetic to their interests, they were at a disadvantage, as the landholders' power was actually being enhanced through their collaboration with the railway.[17]

Anti-Chinese Activity in the Valley

Another more devastating display of naivete on the part of Owen and his pre-progressive colleagues was that their position on opening up the valley to new blood would not allow them to take a position on the Chinese issue that was more vicious than their opponents' position. Any time that the Democrats and machine Republicans felt particularly threatened, they could always claim that the progress Owen desired was progress toward racial equality.

It was no accident that Bernard Murphy was the darling of the Workingmen's Party, despite his wealth. So, while Owen was preoccupied with the economic advance of the valley and spoke of the unpleasant necessity of enduring the Chinese presence because of the importance of their contribution,[18] Steven de Lacy and his Democratic/Workingmen's *Herald* could attack Owen as morally depraved amd un-American. Against this kind of competition, Owen did not stand a chance. The lower-status immigrant constituencies of the first and fourth ward of San Jose continued to support the Murphy family, Rea's machine with the Central Pacific, and thus the status quo, and their support continued to be enhanced by a hate campaign launched against the Chinese.[19]

As the politics of the valley in its early American phase were unsophisticated, so were the attacks on the growing Chinese community. On January 14, 1870, San Jose's Chinatown was totally devastated by fire. Owen was quick to blame the Democrats, although arson was never proven. What *was* clear, however, was that the larger community was less than mournful over the loss. After Owen accused the fire department of sitting by while the structures burned (doing their duty only when nearby St. Joseph's Church was threatened), a fireman responded that his indolence had "purged our city of an abominable nuisance." [20] There were

cases of proven arson, however, perpetrated against non-Chinese individuals who did business with local Chinese.[21] Owen's newspaper printed a number of letters, some purported to be from the Ku Klux Klan, claiming responsibility for various burnings (including that of the Naglee Brandy Distillery and the Methodist Episcopal Church of San Jose, both on the same night in 1869),[22] and warning that others who conducted business of any kind with the Chinese would be similarly dealt with.[23]

Another tactic used by the anti-Chinese elements in the valley was the propounding of the myth of great pestilence among Chinese immigrants to the valley. Photographs of Chinese who were supposedly inflicted with leprosy were distributed throughout San Jose, and when Owen tried to ameliorate the panic, his newspaper was branded as the "leper organ" by Democratic competitor de Lacy.[24] With the passage of the Chinese Exclusion Law of 1882 by the U.S. Congress, however, anti-Chinese activities in the valley subsided and took a more civilized turn. Although there was another burning in 1887, most anti-Asian activity revolved around the Anti-Coolie Club and its strategy of boycotting whites who dealt with the Chinese. When the club threatened to boycott the *Mercury*, a high-minded Owen reminded his detractors that his newspaper had never said a good word about the Chinese themselves, and that if the boycott was launched, he would cease to print the minutes of the club, which always included the names of local businesspersons who were to be boycotted.[25] As if to prove his true patriotism, Owen's *Mercury* ladled out generous helpings of news items unfavorable to the Chinese between

1890 and 1892. These items focused on the activities of Congress in extending the life of the 1882 Chinese Exclusion Act for another ten years, and on Chinese illegal entries.[26]

The Orchard Phase

J.J. Owen was not the only source of pressure to open the valley to new sources of prosperity. As early as 1857, one could find growing in the county 35,000 apple, 25,000 peach, 6,000 pear, 1,300 cherry, and 5,600 fruit trees of other varieties. For the most part, these trees represented an experimental or diversionary sidelight for those who grew them.[27] It was becoming increasingly clear, though, that the soil and climate of the Santa Clara Valley were being squandered on grain crops and livestock that could prosper in less favorable terrain.

And, of course, the railroad opened the possibility of distant markets, especially for the French prune that had been brought to the valley by the Pellier brothers. (Indeed, in recounting the preconditions to the orchard phase, no small contribution would be the expertise of the southern European farmers who had come to the valley, and who recognized its potential as a fruit-growing region.) Apples, whose durability was a major advantage, gave way to the more luxurious dried fruits, and by 1874, San Jose could boast a modern drying plant, the Alden Fruit and Vegetable Preserving Company. In 1876, the firm shipped fifteen tons of dried fruit — only a part of what was to follow.

There were also the successful experiments with canning methods. Dr. James Dawson's famous cookstove preserved 350 cases of fruit in 1871, and by the following year the family had established its orchard cannery at Twenty-First and Julian Streets, and was able to triple its output. Within the next decade, dozens of small canneries were scattered throughout the valley, as the future of the industry looked ever more secure.[28]

Another major factor contributed to the transition to orchards — the abundant and accessible water supply available to the orchardist. Unlike conditions in the central valley, where the difficulty of maintaining sources of irrigation necessitated the continuance of large ventures, a generous water table was at the disposal of Santa Clara Valley orchardists. Thus, it was relatively easy for an investor with modest capital to enter the fruit growing business. Also, because the orchards did not demand year-round attention, they could maintain alternate employment in the off-season.

	Less Than 100 Acres	More Than 100 Acres
1880	721	771
1890	1,427	750
1900	3,057	938
1910	3,096	825
1920	4,390	626
1930	5,616	621

Table 1. Number of Farms in Santa Clara County (by Size), 1880-1930.

That these middle class entrepreneurs entered what had for so long been an agricultural venue reserved for gold rush aristocrats is illustrated by the preceeding table. Although many large enterprises remained, there was a remarkable eightfold increase of smaller operations between 1880 and 1930, with the decade between 1890 and 1900 showing the most dramatic increase.[29]

That this transition to smaller operations was instigated by the shift to fruits and away from grains, is no better illustrated than by the following table. The difference in yields between 1899 and 1909 is astonishing proof of the expeditiousness with which fruit orchards supplanted the less-intensive grain farms.[30]

	Wheat	Barley	Oats
1859	549,195	116,207	17,960
1869	1,188,137	405,575	15,134
1879	648,055	716,860	4,771
1889	282,536	589,303	2,000
1899	175,230	1,392,430	51,048
1909	10,198	200,893	9,424
1919	22,199	85,672	8,123
1929	24,844	51,305	1,322

Table 2. Grain Production in Santa Clara County (in Bushels), 1859-1929.

Maturity of the Orchard Phase

Three major obstacles confronted the full development of the fruit industry as it approached the twentieth century. The first was the under-capitalization of the small canning ventures. It was an excruciating wait from the time that major overhead expenses were incurred and the time payment was received for the pack. Because the canners were so extended by the end of the season, it was often necessary for them to direct their commission agents to dispose of the pack within a few weeks, selling an entire year's stock to their customers. Often, this meant liquidation at any price, and undercutting frequently occurred.

The second obstacle was that at the turn of the century, the idea of putting fruit in cans was alien to most Americans. It was clear to the canners that if they could overcome this barrier, sales would rise exponentially.

The third obstacle to the full development of the fruit industry had to do with the availability of cheap labor. Through the 1870s, the Chinese were crucial to the embryonic fruit industry. Historian Sucheng Chan has estimated, based on the manuscript census, that in the peak harvest season of 1880, 48.2 percent of farm labor in Santa Clara County was performed by Chinese workers.[31] With the victory of the anti-Chinese movement and the passage of the Exclusion Law of 1882, this labor supply was sharply curtailed; thus, it is no surprise that immediately following Chinese exclusion, local fruit growers formed a number of organizations to explore and promote the availability of minority labor sources.[32] The Japanese arrived soon thereafter to what seemed to be the open arms of valley residents,[33] and the new fruit-growing, canning, and peripheral concerns adopted postures and policies that would not make it so easy for extremists to remove their new labor supply. That does not mean, however, that these progressives did not also support measures which rendered that labor supply ever vulnerable to, and ever fearful of, intimidation and exploitation.

Before discussing these newer forms of exploitation, let us discuss the movement of the Japanese into the valley and establish their initial role as migrant laborers.

Footnotes

[1] J.P. Raymond, "California Cereals," in *Transactions of the State Agricultural Society,* Sacramento, 1865, 69. Cited in Jan Otto Marius Broek, *The Santa Clara Valley, California,* N.V.A. Oosthoek's Uitgevers-Mij.: Utrecht, 1932, 76.

[2] E.J. Wickson, *Rural California,* Rural, State and Province Series: New York, 1923, 136.

[3] Eugene Sawyer, *History of Santa Clara County,* Historic Record Company: Los Angeles, 1922, 55.

[4] *San Jose Weekly Mercury,* June 18, 1868, 2.

[5] See, *History of San Benito County,* San Francisco, 1881.

[6] Prior to 1864, those who raised crops were required to "enclose their lands with good and substantial fences, or otherwise submit to the depredations of the stock, without any legal address." Broek, *Santa Clara Valley,* 61.

[7] Broek, *Santa Clara Valley,* 61.

[8] Kevin Starr, *Americans and the California Dream: 1850-1915,* Oxford University Press: New York, 1973, 192.

[9] *San Jose Weekly Mercury,* April 15, 1880, 2.

[10] Elmer Clarence Sandmeyer, *The Anti-Chinese Movement in California,* University of Illinois Press: Chicago, 1973, 42 ff.

[11] Ping Chiu, *Chinese Labor in California,* State Historical Society of Wisconsin: Madison, 1967, 40 ff.

[12] See, Peter C.Y. Leung, *One Day, One Dollar: Locke, California and the Chinese Farming Experience in the Sacramento Delta,* Chinese American History Project: El Cerrito, CA, 1984.

[13] Sucheng Chan, "The Chinese in California Agriculture," unpubl. manuscript, 40.

[14] Broek, *Santa Clara Valley,* 69.

[15] Glenna Matthews, "A California Middletown: The Social History of San Jose in the Depression," unpubl. Ph.D. dissertation, Stanford University, 1976, 29.

[16] In order to attract new settlers, Owen was constantly marketing the valley in flyers and booklets which were sent back east. A common theme was that despite what people might have heard, there still was land available, and for a fair price. In fact, Owen's importunement reflected a constant concern that land prices were too high, with the large owners grabbing more than their share. Historians have argued that a major hinderance to further settlement of California was the difficulty of buying land. See Carey McWilliams, *Factories in the Field,* Peregrine Publishers, Inc.: Santa Barbara, 1971 edition, 11-27.

[17] Perhaps the most important link between the Central Pacific and the local land barons involved the Rea family of Gilroy. In return for maintaining the railroad's interest in San Jose, the family was blessed with a major junction on their South Bay properties (increasing land values by about 1,000 percent, *San Jose Mercury,* February 10, 1870), and a position on the state's railroad commission for James Rea.

[18] Owen writes: "...the labor which we employ them to perform would go unperformed if prevailing rates for white labor were required to be paid for that class of work. On the other hand we think it can be shown that the white laborer is actually benefitted, and the sphere of his opportunities for employment actually enlarged by the employment of Chinese labor." *San Jose Mercury,* March 4, 1869.

[19] Denis Kearney was a frequent visitor to San Jose, and he never failed to draw a large and boistrous crowd. The Workingmen's Party had a strong following in the valley.

[20] *San Jose Weekly Mercury,* January 20, 1870, 3.

[21] *San Jose Weekly News,* April 22, 1869, 3.

[22] Naglee employed Chinese workers in his operation, and the church had recently opened a school for Chinese children. See *San Jose Weekly Mercury,* February 25, 1869, 2.

[23] See the *San Jose Weekly Mercury,* March 11, 1869, April 22, 1869, November 4, 1869, and May 20, 1869.

[24] *Daily Morning Times* (San Jose), February 21, 1883.

[25] *San Jose Mercury,* March 30, 1886.

[26] See, the following issues of the *San Jose Daily Mercury:* April 16, 1890; May 2, 1890; May 22, 1890; June 1,

1890; July 19, 1890; August 6, 1890; February 1, 1891; August 17, 1891; October 10, 1891; December 11, 1891; January 4, 1892; January 25, 1892; February 20, 1892; April 2, 1892; April 13, 1892; April 23, 1892; April 26, 1892; May 4, 1892; and May 5, 1892.

[27] *State Register,* 1859, 241. Cited in Broek, *Santa Clara Valley,* 67.

[28] San Jose Chamber of Commerce, *Santa Clara County, California,* Wright–Eley Company: San Jose, 1930, 37, 38.

[29] Broek, *Santa Clara Valley,* 124.

[30] Broek, *Santa Clara Valley,* 65.

[31] Chan, "Chinese in California Agriculture," Table 3, 42.

[32] See Matthews, "California Middletown," *passim.*

[33] The *Mercury* called the new immigrants "very polite and urbane as is their characteristic." *San Jose Mercury,* December 18, 1898, 7.

Sakura
CHERRY

CHAPTER 3
JAPANESE MIGRANT LABOR, 1895-1907

The first Japanese farmers arrived in the Santa Clara Valley in the mid-1890s. Their appearance during the orchard phase of the valley's development was not accidental. Like the Chinese before them, the Japanese were drawn by the opportunities for work and were welcomed as long as they supplied useful labor. Japanese migrants, thus, along with the Chinese, supplied much of the required labor for the transition to an orchard economy.

Labor Flows:
From Chinese to Japanese

As in most other counties in California, the Chinese arrived before the Japanese. Their numbers swelled with the need for labor, finally reaching a crest during the 1880s and 1890s. The anti-Chinese movement that engulfed the state during this period threatened to extinguish the fragile bachelor society ensconced in San Jose's Chinatown. Just as surely as the Chinese were being driven out, the Japanese were being drawn in. The numbers in the following table are derived from census figures, but do not include Chinese and Japanese seasonal workers whose presence in the valley was only for portions of the year, which was, at peak times, considerable.

Year	Chinese	Japanese
1860	22	—
1870	1,525	—
1880	2,695	—
1890	2,723	27
1900	1,738	284
1910	1,064	2,299
1920	839	2,981
1930	761	4,320
1940	555	4,049

Table 3.
Chinese and Japanese in Santa Clara County, 1860-1940.

While the broad pattern of Chinese and Japanese migration was predictable, the precise way in which Japanese migrant labor replaced Chinese migrant labor was governed by the peculiarities of the industry concerned. The best example is shown in the seed farms in the county. In 1908, the total value of farm and dairy products in the county was $8,389,680. Of that, $5,175,010 derived from deciduous fruit; $1,055,00 from cereals, hay, dairy, etc.; $1,043,670 from vegetables; and $116,000 from berries. Seed farms accounted for a significant $1,000,000 of the total.[1] Seed farms grew carefully selected garden stock, which in turn was used to produce seeds. Through careful care, irrigation and cultivation, and the removal of all undesirable strains, the quality of the seeds was determined.

Generally, seed farms required two kinds of labor: work with teams and hand work. The skilled work was almost invariably reserved for white men who plowed, cultivated, and hauled. These were paid between $35 and $50 per month with board and lodging, while those employed in supervisory capacities were paid from $50 to $65 and more a month. At the lower end, Chinese and Japanese were hired for the intensive work of caring for the seed stock. Their wages ranged from $0.80 to $1.75 per day usually including lodging but without board. Since boarding costs were equivalent to $12 to $15 per month and white workers were paid by the month while Asian workers were paid by the number of days worked, the gap in salaries between white and Asian workers was significant.[2] Wage labor discrimination was thus achieved through the distinction of skilled versus unskilled labor, restricting the former to white workers.

On the seed farms of Santa Clara Valley, Japanese labor did not displace Chinese labor during this period. Rather, the industry as a whole sought to keep as many Chinese workers as it could. As the numbers of Chinese in the valley dwindled, however, the seed farms initially were forced to hire white men to fill their labor needs; later, they brought in Japanese workers to replace the white laborers. During the 1880s, the Chinese practically supplied all the hand labor for the valley's seed farms. Around 1900, with the flight of the Chinese and the expansion of the industry, white men, chiefly Portuguese and Italians, were employed. The experiment failed because, "It was more inconvenient to obtain them [white men] than it had been to obtain the Chinese, because they were not organized into groups, did not remain on the ranch year after year as the typical Chinese had

done, and were not so skillful in their work."[3]

Japanese laborers became available at about that time and soon replaced the white men. They were preferred to the white men because they were organized into work gangs under bosses like the Chinese. However, they proved less desirable than the Chinese. "They are easily attracted by more remunerative work elsewhere, with the result that if their demands are not satisfactorily met the labor force becomes depleted. Moreover, they are less attentive and less careful in their work, do not look to the employer's interests as do the Chinese, and require more supervision."[4] As a result, the managers of seed farms in 1908 kept a mixed labor force of white ethnics as teamsters and supervisors, and Chinese and Japanese, the latter in greater numbers, for hand work.

A similar situation prevailed in the fruit packing houses where Chinese men constituted the preferred source of labor. For about thirty years (until about 1903), the Chinese did all of the packing of green fruit. When their numbers declined, white women were hired. In this instance, apparently, the relative scarcity of Chinese men and their attractiveness resulted in closing the discriminatory wage gap. "The Chinese have always been regarded as the best packers," reported the Immigration Commission in 1908, "and in order to retain as many of them as possible in employment their wages have been raised from time to time, until now . . . [their wages] are not much less than those paid to white women working as packers and the white men working as laborers." Still, in 1908, white women were paid an average of $1.82 for a ten-hour day, while Chinese men received $1.75 for an eleven-hour day. Portuguese and Irish men, in contrast, were paid from $2.00 to $2.50 for an eleven-hour day.[5]

The orchards of Santa Clara Valley posed the exception as far as Chinese labor was concerned. Here, their declining numbers eventually led to their complete displacement from this field of labor by white women and children and Japanese men. Part of the difficulty that the Chinese encountered stemmed from the orchardists' desire to obtain labor gangs or organized groups to do the work. They would thus hire persons who could secure those groups, such as Japanese labor contractors or Italians who would buy the entire crop on the trees. Thus, on the 13 orchards visited in June and July of 1908, the Immigration Commission found 351 persons employed. Of these, 46 were white men; 66, white women; and 47, white children. Of the remaining 192, 187 were Japanese men and 5 were Japanese women.[6] The flow of orchard labor, accordingly, had moved from Chinese to Japanese.

Still, the process by which the Japanese replaced Chinese farm laborers in the valley was accomplished incrementally and the timing varied from industry to industry. The Chinese and Japanese, in fact, were contemporaries, and, especially during the period of migrant labor, the Japanese migrant community came to resemble the bachelor society of its predecessor.

Migrant Labor and Impermanence

One of the characteristics of migrant labor and the bachelor society was its impermanence. Chinese and Japanese laborers were desirable because of their mobility, arriving when their labor was needed and leaving when their task was accomplished. The orchards and gardens of the Santa Clara Valley beckoned Japanese migrant laborers during the last decade of the nineteenth century. Very little is known about this first group of Issei, or first-generation, Japanese farmers. It seems likely, however, that they were following the farm-labor paths pioneered by the Chinese during the 1860s and 1870s and by Japanese during the late 1880s. The paths led from San Francisco to the valleys of the interior, and essentially offered two roads for Asian migrants. The first followed the rivers eastward through the Vaca Valley and into the Sacramento delta. The second path led southward, down the peninsula to the Santa Clara Valley and from there branched off into the coastal valleys of Salinas and San Luis Obispo, or headed southeast toward Fresno.

The direction taken by the migrants, in fact, was largely determined by the seasons and crops. Thus, Issei migrant laborers worked at strawberries in the Santa Clara Valley from April through June, remained for the apricot, pear, and prune harvest during July and August, and packed up and moved on to Fresno for grapes in late August and September. When Hisao Omori and his younger brother, Tomoyuki, arrived in San Jose in 1913, they discovered that their father, Kotaro, was in Salinas. They met him there, and later that year, returned to the Santa Clara Valley to harvest prunes.[7] Even the movement of Japanese laborers in the Santa Clara Valley itself was governed by the crops. Thus, Yoshio Ando recalled how Japanese migrants picked strawberries in Alviso during April, moved to the middle and far ends of the valley to the apricot and prune orchards in July and August, and later traveled on to Fresno to pick grapes.[8]

Legend

[ ] indicates boardinghouse locations
1. Teramoto, advisor
2. Japanese Association Hall
   Iida Sake Brewery
3. Italian homes
4. Hagihara Sewing School
[5.] Sanryo-yokan
6. Eeki Dry Goods
7. Nakamoto Dry Goods
8. [A] Shiba Roominghouse
   B Shiba Watchmaker
9. Dokuritsu Bukyo-kai (Independent Buddhist Church)
   1st Floor — Japanese Language School/Childcare Center
   2nd Floor — Temple
[10.] Nankaya-yokan
   (owned by Kinaga)
[11.] A Okita Grocery
   [B] 1st Floor — Taihei-yokan Poolroom
      2nd Floor — Taihei-yokan Boardinghouse
      3rd Floor — Akashi Photo
12. Nishiura Bath-house/Poolhall
13. Ishino Photo
14. Tanabe Candystore
15. Anzai Barbershop
16. Arita Watch and Jewelry Store
17. Arita Bicycle
18. Kawakami Shoten (books, candy, etc.)
19. Kajiwo Poolhall
20. Sakura-yu (bath-house/poolhall)
21. Hosokawa Tailor
22. Shiraishi Restaurant
23. Shiroma Fishmarket
[24.] Saikai-yokan
   (owned by Tsuida)
[25.] Tokiwa-yokan
   (owned by Sakamoto)
26. Geishu-ya Manju Shop
   (owned by Kuzaka)
27. Nomitsu Tofu
28. Canton Restaurant
29. Nishiura Butcher
30. Yabuki Poolhall
31. Tuc Woo (market)
32. 5-6 gambling houses; 2 restaurants
33. Yachio-tei (bar)
34. Izuno home

[35.] Yamaguchi-yokan
36. Chinese home
37. A Maeda Barbershop
   [B] Maeda Roominghouse
38. Matsunoya (bar)
39. Sashi-shokai (market)
40. Minato-yu (bath-house)
41. Ishimaru Barbershop
42. 1st Floor — Inouye Grocery
   2nd Floor — Imada Photo
43. Baseball Field/Sumo Wrestling
44. San Jose Bukyo-kai (Buddhist Church)
45. Italian Winery
46. Japanese Hall (community center)
47. Tokunaga Dry Goods/Drugs
48. Kinokunia Dry Goods (till 1912)
   Ishikawa Dry Goods (after 1912)
[49.] Kyushu-ya Roominghouse
50. Tsunashima Soda Water
51. Miyako-tei (bar)
52. Dobashi Company
53. Mitsunaga Transfer (transportation)
54. Iwasaki Tailor
55. Iwasa Shoe Repair
56. Ishikawa Music Store
[57.] Toyo Boardinghouse (till 1911)
   Japanese Association Bldg. (after 1911)
58. Tabata Garage
59. A Mrs. Hori, midwife
   [B] Mrs. Hori's Boardinghouse
60. Wesleyan Methodist Church
61. Dr. Fukui (office)
62. Japanese Hospital
63. Mrs. Seki, midwife
64. Takaichi and Kimura, advisors
[65.] San Jose Boardinghouse
   (owned by Sakamoto)

Structures Still Standing Today:
46. Japanese Hall
59. Hori Midwife/Boardinghouse
62. Japanese Hospital

Businesses/Organizations Currently Operating Today:
44. Buddhist Church
52. Dobashi Company (Market)
60. Wesleyan Methodist Church

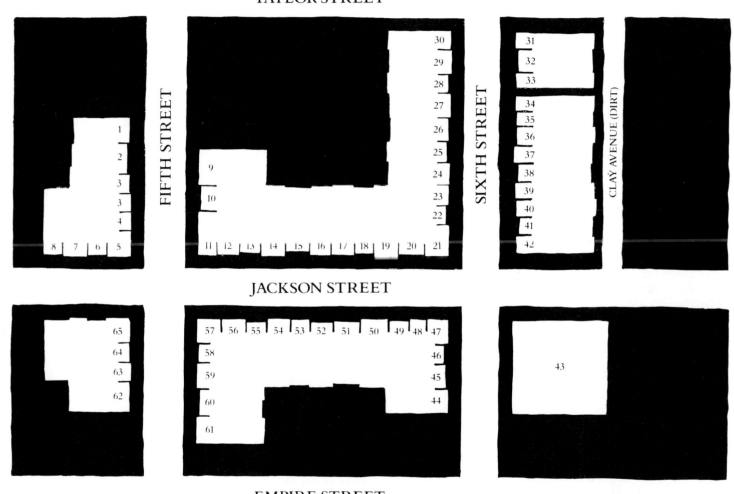

Located just north of downtown San Jose, Nihonmachi was the center of Japanese community life. The town emerged as a group of boardinghouses for the arriving immigrants and migrant farm laborers.

San Jose Nihonmachi 1910–1920

Bunkhouses, Chinatown, and Nihonmachi

Because of the scarcity of documentary evidence, we can only offer an informed conjecture on certain features of early Issei migrant labor in the valley. At first, it appears that Japanese labor was unorganized. Workers arrived by barge from San Francisco at Alviso, where they were greeted by white farmers who recruited the migrants for work on their ranches.[9] Probably, then, the Issei would remain on those ranches in bunkhouses provided by the landowners for the duration of the harvest. No doubt these men occasionally ventured to San Jose's Chinatown seeking out the delectable pleasures of food and drink, women, and gambling. By 1902, a matter of a few years, that social grouping formed the nucleus of a Nihonmachi or Japantown — wooden structures erected next to the brick buildings of Chinatown on Sixth Street.

Perhaps among the first structures of that Nihonmachi were the "Japanese camps" described by historian Yamato Ichihashi. These later evolved into the boardinghouses that came to typify the early town. The "camps," wrote Ichihashi, were "bunkhouses of the cheapest sort" in which the men "slept, ate, and sought from the bosses work in the district."[10] The "camps," accordingly, represented a higher stage of labor organization, that of bosses and gangs. This, of course, was preferred by the white landowners and enabled the Japanese to replace the Chinese migrants, especially in the valley's orchards, and to compete with white women and children in the picking aspect of that work. In that sense, perhaps, Nihonmachi was the creation of the Santa Clara Valley's developing industrial agriculture. More assuredly, Nihonmachi served the valley's fields and orchards — at first the white owners, and later the Japanese tenants.

That fact was exhibited in the nature of Nihonmachi itself. During this period of migrant labor, Nihonmachi was not a residential community — it was primarily a temporary boarding area for transitory men. In 1902, for instance, the San Jose area held several hundred Japanese residents and an additional 3,000 seasonal workers who swelled the local population during the spring and summer months.[11] The kinds of businesses established, consequently, catered to the needs of migrant labor. Accordingly, boardinghouses were a prominent feature of the town, along with allied structures such as bathhouses, poolhalls, gambling parlors, and houses of prostitution. Even as late as 1910, Nihonmachi maintained eleven boardinghouses, three bathhouses, and five poolhalls. The map of Nihonmachi on page 23 illustrates that configuration.

Migrant laborers, thus, constituted the lifeblood of the town. Masuo Akizuki recalled those early times:

When I came to San Jose the day after my arrival, everybody was working in the countryside. The boarding houses in San Jose Japantown found jobs for us. They brought us by horse carriage to the place to work, and we each were given one blanket. Our living conditions were miserable at that time. We slept next to a horse stable on our blankets and some straw. It was so miserable Sansei [third-generation Japanese Americans] may not be able to believe it. When we finished the work, we went back to the boarding house and rested there until the next job came around.[12]

Nihonmachi was indeed a kind of ghetto. It was a relatively densely populated area, especially during harvest time, that was segregated from the rest of the city. Together with Chinatown, the location housed the vast majority of Asian residents of San Jose. Most importantly, perhaps, Nihonmachi was a labor reserve for the farms and orchards of the valley.

Saké, Fisticuffs, and Gambling

The days were not idyllic. The period of migrant labor was typified by the bachelor society of young men, alienated from the wider society in a foreign land. Further, they were strangers to one another despite having come from the same districts *(ken)* in Japan, and were living in an unfamiliar social order not based on the Japanese family or kinship group. Moreover, they faced the daily rigors of the life of a migrant, moving from boardinghouse to barn, from Alviso to Fresno, from sunup to sundown. Migrant labor society was neither ordinary nor simple. *Saké* [Japanese rice wine], fisticuffs, and gambling exemplified some of the realities of this period of Japanese farming in the Santa Clara Valley.

Those behaviors should not be viewed as happenings during quaint pioneer days nor as mere aberrations arising from a rough and wild era. Rather, they constituted characteristic, albeit tragic, consequences of the established social relations in the Santa Clara political economy. The Issei migrant laborers were indeed victims. But their conduct, while understandable within the context of exploitation, also point to universal human frailties and reveal the Japanese farmers in all their humanness — warts and all. News items in the *San Jose Mercury* helped to reveal this darker side of the Japanese experience in the valley. Caution, nonetheless, must be exercised in reading these news accounts. The *Mercury* clearly highlighted negative aspects of Asian Americans during this period and associated them with, among other stereotypes, criminal behavior. Still, although the documentation is not an accurate or complete portrayal of the bachelor society, it illustrates anti-social responses to victimization.

Conflicts between Japanese men were commonly reported in the newspaper. In fact, one of the earliest mentions of Japanese in the valley appeared in the May 28, 1895, issue of the *Mercury* under the heading, "Joyful Japanese." The story noted that too much red wine and talk of war between Japan and China led to a drunken brawl. On November 8, 1902, the *Mercury* reported under the by-line, "Japanese Laborer Creates Disturbance," that a Japanese man very much under the influence of alcohol caused a disturbance, bordering on violence, at the train station. In a note of defiance, the man refused to give his name or address. Other reported conflicts included the shooting of I. Ikaha [sic], proprietor of a boardinghouse, by an unknown assailant,[13] and large fights termed "riots" by the newspaper. The *Mercury* of April 26, 1908, reported that the night before, a "jui jitsu fight" broke out in Nihonmachi and the riot police were called. When they arrived, everyone had vanished. On October 6, 1908, the *Mercury* carried a story of a "riot and panic" in the Japanese theater caused by nine Japanese from Alaska. During the disturbance, a man was slashed with knives. Another stabbing occurred when men from a Japanese "press gang" came to San Jose to recruit laborers for Alaska. Apparently, after refusing to go, a Mr. Imafuji attacked Mr. Tominaga with a knife, seriously wounding the latter.[14]

The newspaper reported several thefts among Japanese during this period. On February 3, 1905, the *Mercury* reported that S. Hata and K. Kawahara were charged with fighting, during which the former sustained a serious head wound. The fight apparently was triggered by Kawahara's allegation that Hata had stolen his coat and $5. In another incident, two Japanese men, employees of the Fox Nurseries on Milpitas Road, were charged with robbery, as reported in the December 11, 1905, *Mercury*. They were identified by their victims, K. Nomise, K. Okuno, and K. Kanikami [sic]. On July 14, 1908, the *Mercury* reported that a Japanese man had been arrested for stealing a watch at a pawn shop, and, more spectacularly, the December 28, 1908, issue contained the head-line, "Japanese Attempts to Hold Up San Jose Bank." F. Kawamura, it reported, a "notorious highbinder" (gang member) wanted for murder in Alaska and Sacramento, attempted to rob the Japanese bank in Chinatown. He was caught and placed in jail.

"Jap Gamblers Rounded Up in Big Police Raid," read the July 12, 1908, edition of the *Mercury*. The raid netted twenty-seven Japanese and two whites for gambling at 610 North Fifth Street. The two white men, George Price and E.G. Richie, were charged with conducting a gambling game, and the Japanese each paid a $10 bail. On November 24, 1909, the *Mercury* reported that a Japanese man was

found murdered in Nihonmachi. He had been stabbed six times. The tip of a thumb was found near the man's body. A suspect, his thumb bandaged and his clothes covered with blood, was soon arrested. The paper concluded that no motive was known but that the victim was a gambler and the murder took place after the closing of a lottery house. O. Yama, a known gambler according to the *Mercury* of October 14, 1909, was attacked and badly beaten by fifteen Japanese in Nihonmachi. Yama refused to identify his assailants or their motives to police. The police, however, felt that the beating had taken place "over a woman."

Gender Relations

Conflicts over women were not infrequent in the bachelor society. For instance, the July 28, 1908, issue of the *Mercury* reported that S. Sakato shot and killed Hisagi Yamamoto. Yamamoto, according to the story, had been infatuated with Sakato's wife for two years. During that time, Sakato learned that Yamamoto plotted to kill both him and his wife. On the day of his death, Yamamoto threatened to carry out his plan. He pointed a gun at Sakato's wife after professing his love for her. Sakato, in turn, drew his gun and killed Yamamoto. Sakato was exonerated of all blame.

A story in the October 14, 1902, issue of the *Mercury* revealed not only a shooting but also the presence of a white prostitute. According to the article, there was a "Japanese resort" at 622 North Second Street. Here, "For their entertainment there are many things of interest and...many things to get their money." Among these "things of interest" was a white woman. Kobashe and Kayi [sic], it seems, got into an argument over the woman, during which Kobashe hit Kayi. Kayi then drew a revolver and began shooting, injuring Kobashe and another Japanese. Apparently, white women served as prostitutes to Asian men in San Jose's Chinatown and Nihonmachi. The *Mercury* reported in its May 28, 1908, issue the arrest of a white woman, Mrs. C.N. Franklin of Monterey, during a police raid of suspected houses of prostitution in Chinatown. According to the story, her husband had set her up in a house there and was arrested in a nearby boardinghouse. We can only offer a conjecture on what Franklin was doing in the boardinghouse; he was perhaps soliciting customers.

Conflicts: Oppression and Resistance

Not all conflicts, however, were indicative of anti-social behavior. On the contrary, many were noble acts of courage striking back at oppression, whether emanating from whites or Japanese. Thus, for example, the April 9, 1908, *Mercury* reported that Fue Yamashita, wife of a Japanese farmer for two years, filed for a divorce on the grounds of continued cruelty.[15] The husband claimed that she was being kidnapped. As far as we know, this was the first divorce case involving Japanese in the Santa Clara Valley. The instance is particularly notable because it was initiated by a woman despite the Meiji norm of male dominance, and because separation was pursued in the American courts. (We will document the overwhelming number of divorces initiated by Japanese women in our discussion on the period of dependency in Chapter Five.) A more common type of notice appeared

later that year in the *Mercury:* the wife of Y. Ewata [sic] had left him to live with another Japanese man, a Mr. Une who worked at a Japanese store on Sixth Street and Jackson.[16]

Besides intra-Japanese conflicts, Japanese migrants were the target of physical abuse by the valley's white residents. The newspaper offers glimpses of such attacks along with instances in which the Japanese fought back. According to a *Mercury* story of January 11, 1902, T. Imano, a Japanese laborer, filed charges in court against L.P. Pfeiffenberg. Imano alleged that the defendant and two other boys "threw bricks at his horse and caused his animal to run away." Witnesses, however, contradicted Imano's claim and placed the blame instead on two Chinese. The complaint, the account concluded, would be dropped. Still, Imano's suit stands as a protest against indignity.

In another incident, five Japanese men on their way to prayer service at the First Presbyterian Church were beaten by five white men before a crowd of about a hundred onlookers. The Japanese started running and about fifty whites joined in the chase. When the police arrived, oddly enough, the five Japanese victims were arrested and not their assailants. After about five days, the case against the Japanese men was dismissed because of lack of evidence.[17] On May 9, 1908, the *Mercury* reported that Charles Snow, the fourteen-year-old son of Mr. and Mrs. Fred Snow of Agnew, was in critical condition as a result of blows to the head by an "excited Japanese." While the newspaper did not assign motives except to suggest that the accused was drunk, the attack on young Snow may have been prompted by more substantive reasons.

Better documented was the killing of John Kyne,

a Southern Pacific foreman and San Jose resident, in Peterville just south of Gilroy. According to the newspaper accounts, ill feeling existed between Kyne and the men working under him. Four Japanese workers assaulted Kyne on November 3, 1908; Kyne died later in the sanitarium from his wounds. J. Kemgji [sic] was arrested for Kyne's murder after fleeing south to San Benito via a handcar. In March of the following year, another of the men, Torahiko Yoshimizu, was arrested in Salt Lake City for the killing of Kyne.[18] It seems reasonable to surmise that the killing of Kyne was prompted by genuine grievances held by Japanese workers. There seemed to have been little other recourse to striking a blow at their immediate tormentor. Such was the lot of laborers whose status as perpetual aliens and migrants separated them from ordinary means of redress or even the rights of citizenship.

Japanese workers in the Santa Clara Valley also resorted to collective protest. The May 20, 1904, issue of the *Mercury* reported, "Sensational Strike of Japs at Santa Clara." The story recounted the events of May 18:

> The vicinity of the depot presented a very busy appearance this morning, the occasion being a strike among the twenty Japanese who have been here for the past two months in the employ of the Southern Pacific railroad company. It appears that one of the Japanese workmen had too much to say about the war during working hours. He accomplished little work and was discharged. The other Japanese demanded that their countryman should be put back to work, and on being refused they all quit work. A Japanese peacemaker arrived from San Francisco during the day and attempted to adjust matters, but to no avail, and the places made vacant by the Japs was [sic] soon filled by a gang of white men.

Still, the price paid by Japanese workers for striking was their jobs. At least in this instance, troublesome Japanese labor became quickly dispensible.

The February 19, 1908, issue of the *Mercury* reported that Annie Johnson had eloped with a Japanese man to Vancouver. Johnson, the story noted, was a San Jose domestic worker.[19] That same year, on April 4, the *Mercury* reported the attempt of I. Nakano and S. Hasakawa [sic] to break the motor-tandem speed record from Watsonville to San Jose. The pair whizzed through Gilroy at a speed exceeding 35 miles per hour — too fast for Constable Jack White to catch. "He endeavored to halt them and place them under arrest, but they went by him like the wind, leaving him enveloped in a cloud of dust. . . ." Constable Jack telephoned the San Jose police who set up a road block on Monterey Road near Edenvale and in that way finally managed to stop and arrest the two men.

Another account involves the adventures and mishaps of one I. Nakano, proprietor of a bicycle shop on Sixth Street in Nihonmachi and the nemesis of Constable Jack of Gilroy. Nakano, the July 9, 1908, issue of the *Mercury* reported, bought a motorcycle with a powerful racing engine. Promptly, he rear-ended a wagon at high speed, breaking his leg. A week after spending six weeks in the hospital, Nakano rounded a corner too fast, hit a wet spot, and went into a skid. "When he finally stopped a toboggan slide on one ear, at least half of that member was missing in addition to several square inches of skin from other portions of his anatomy." His third accident involved a crash with another motorcycle and "only the presence of Police Officer Laderich saved the little Jap from a beating at the hands of the other motorcyclist." Nakano paid for the repair of both bikes (about $75), but he was not finished yet. On the long stretches of road between Watsonville and San Jose, Nakano opened up his machine and again, as he breezed through Gilroy, all that Constable Jack could see was "a brown streak." The telephone rang at the San Jose police station, a roadblock was set up on Monterey Road, and Nakano was waved down with guns. He was fined $20 for speeding.

In the final analysis, it matters little whether Annie Johnson and her unnamed Japanese lover eloped in a fit of passion, or whether their act was a triumph of class solidarity over racial distinctions. Similarly, it matters little whether I. Nakano and S. Hasakawa were half-crazed speed demons, or whether they were early mechanical geniuses. For in the end, they were all exhibiting bits of humanity, flashes of self-determination. And in so doing, they not only asserted their individual selves; they speak to us today of boardinghouses littered with broken dreams, and of orchards awaiting the spring.

The Drive for Permanence

The humdrum daily work of Japanese farmers in the orchards and fields of Santa Clara Valley was no less real or heroic. At first, Nihonmachi and the surrounding farms in the valley formed a single continuum of labor flows. Periodically, Japanese men living in the boardinghouses would leave for various farms, taking with them a blanket. When that job was finished, they would return to await another farm summons. Gradually, however, pockets of Japanese settlements began popping up throughout the valley at Alviso, Agnew, Berryessa, Milpitas, and in the Trimble Road areas. These Japanese farming communities or clusters in different areas of the valley were quite distinctive from Nihonmachi. In fact, the contrasting features of the clusters and Nihonmachi resulted in a sense of separation — the former characterized by families with a greater degree of permanence, and the latter typified by migrant single men.

For many of the valley's Japanese farmers, work began in the plantations of Hawaii. Of the nine earliest Japanese farming families interviewed, six of them came to San Jose as re-migrants from Hawaii.[20] Yoshio Ando's family history provides a good example of this pattern. Hidekichi and Miyo Ando migrated from Hiroshima, Japan, to Oahu, Hawaii, in 1892. They worked on the sugar plantations there until 1904 when the family sailed to San Francisco seeking better opportunities. Upon arrival in San Francisco, Hidekichi heard of job prospects in San Jose and thus traveled south. He found work in the prune orchards of a Mr. Irish in the Willow Glen area. Here Hidekichi, Miyo, and their son lived in a two-room structure along with several Japanese bachelors, the family occupying one of the rooms. Miyo cooked for the family and the bachelor workers, and Hidekichi helped the men find jobs and recruited additional laborers for the Irish orchards from the boardinghouses in Nihonmachi. By 1909, Hidekichi was able to begin sharecropping prunes with a Mr. Kirk on Dry Creek Road. His movement from migrant laborer to sharecropper was probably facilitated by his role as labor boss.[21]

Another way of advancing to tenancy was through arrangements with a former employer. Harry Araki's family illustrates that method. Suyetaro and Chiyo Araki migrated from Hiroshima to Hawaii where Suyetaro worked as a domestic to a white family. His employer recommended that Suyetaro go to California for better opportunities. Taking that advice, Suyetaro moved to Sacramento and then to San Jose. Here he was joined by Chiyo at Wayne Station where Suyetaro worked for R.D. Fox at the Fox Nurseries.

The Fox Nurseries was established in 1852 on Milpitas Road and during the late nineteenth century was the largest nursery on the West Coast. Its founder, B.S. Fox, was credited with developing some of the finest varieties of pears, and the nurseries played an important role in the development of the valley's orchards.[22] At the Fox Nurseries, Suyetaro gained valuable knowledge of orchard trees and used the information later when he had his own orchards and began growing bareroot stock for sale. Sometime before 1904, Suyetaro began farming on about five acres of the Fox ranch.

Partnerships were another means of achieving landed status. That strategy is exhibited in the family histories of Shigio Masunaga and Eiichi Sakauye. Takematsu Masunaga was a remarkable man. He was born in Kokawa, Wakayama *ken* in 1869. At the age of nineteen, Takematsu sailed for San Francisco, arriving in 1888. He worked as a domestic in Alameda, as a farmhand on the hop ranches in Sacramento, and as a cook in San Jose. In 1892, Takematsu returned to Japan to start a lumber business only to have it fail after a few years. He returned to America in 1895, worked as a farm laborer at Wright Station in the Santa Cruz mountains and as a cook for a white family, and eventually started a bamboo art shop at 85 San Fernando Street in San Jose. He left the business after two years and worked as a farm laborer in Salinas, as a cook for a family in San Jose, and as an employee of the Gallagher Fruit Company in Alviso. In the early 1900s, Takematsu helped organize the Kino Company, a group of about half a dozen bachelors and a few families, all from Wakayama *ken*. (The company's name derived from the Kii Peninsula of Wakayama.) With its pooled resources, the Kino Company was able to lease several acres of land on the Able ranch in the Trimble Road area along the banks of the Coyote Creek. Here the members farmed strawberries and garden vegetables till about 1910 when the company probably disbanded.[23]

Yuwakichi Sakauye was no less remarkable. He, like Takematsu Masunaga, hailed from Wakayama *ken*. Yuwakichi arrived in Seattle in early 1900 where he worked on the railroad. In the spring of that year, he moved south to Wright Station where fruits such as pears, plums, and cherries were carried by train to Los Gatos. After sharecropping strawberries on North First Street for about a year, Yuwakichi formed a partnership with two other men from Wakayama, Kino and Nakamura, around 1902. They called their group the NKS Company from the last names of the three partners.[24] We are unable to determine whether the NKS Company preceded the formation of the Kino Company or vice versa. In any case, both began about the same time, both were started by people from Wakayama, and both were located in the Trimble Road area. The Kino and NKS companies were extraordinary because they were formed so early in the period of Japanese migrant labor in the valley, and because they are good illustrations of ethnic cooperation on the basis of *ken*. They also point to the beginnings of how clusters were probably formed — by groups of farmers from the same *ken* or, in most cases, by groups of friends.

Agnew: An Example of an Early Farm Cluster

The cluster at Agnew is the best documented example of an early farm cluster. In 1908, the Immigration Commission conducted a study of the community. In that year, according to the Commission, the two largest clusters of Japanese farming communities in the valley were at Alviso and Agnew, some eight and six miles north of San Jose, respectively, on the southern littoral of the bay. Alviso, due east of Agnew, was by far the larger of the two, numbering about forty-four Japanese farmers, while Agnew held about one-third that amount. The cluster at Agnew was widely separated rather than grouped on a single tract of land. The first Japanese farmers arrived in Agnew in 1901; most settled after 1905. The early date is significant because while the vast majority of Japanese in the valley were migrant laborers on white farms, a settled Japanese farming community was growing.

The Commission studied twenty of the farms in Agnew and Alviso, which were selected as typical

of the small farms in the area. Those twenty farmers leased 235 acres, the largest tract being 47 acres, the smallest, 2 acres. The average holding was 11.75 acres. Some of the larger tracts were leased under the names of several persons, then subdivided and subleased to others either on a cash or share basis. Rents paid varied from $10 to $20 per acre, and averaged $15.35 per acre. Most of the farmers grew vegetables or berries, especially strawberries, although there were a few orchards and dairy cattle. Sales for 1907 totaled $23,624.22, and receipts in 1908 amounted to $6,680 from strawberries, $12,500 from other berries, $1,565 from vegetables, and $2,879 from other crops.[25]

Highly intensive farming was performed, with very little investment in the latest farm equipment. "These farmers do not keep any live stock except horses and very few of them; for after the land is once plowed and furrowed so as to make the ridges for plants and the irrigating trenches, all of the work is done by hand with hoe, weeding knife, and a few other hand tools of the simplest kind."[26] The farmers maximized their labor by farming as a household unit, including the labor of wives, and as collectives through "swap work." Most, thus, did not require additional labor except for those with the largest holdings during the harvest time, and except for white teamsters who were contracted to break the ground. All of those strategies enabled land tenancy with a minimum of capital. Other tactics included the construction of small "shacks" to serve as houses, and the use of every available piece of land including the ridges along the irrigation ditches, which were planted with vegetables consumed by the farmers themselves. While admirable, Japanese intensive farming was not indicative of successful farming per se; on the contrary, it revealed the difficult struggle waged by Japanese farmers against the impermanence of migrant labor.

There are several interesting features in the pattern of settlement. These, if typical, shed new light on the conventional notions of Japanese involvement in California agriculture. First, most of these farmers, sixteen of the twenty-three, were married before arriving in California; thirteen of these came as couples. Of crucial importance here is not the presence of women in the bachelor society, but the presence of women in the movement of Japanese from migrant laborers to tenant farmers. Women were employed on the farm and in the cannery at Alviso. That labor probably made Japanese tenancy possible, or at least, more likely. Second, a majority arrived as re-migrants from Hawaii, eleven of twenty farmers. "A large number had, after marriage, gone to Hawaii as laborers upon the sugar plantations, and then upon tiring of life there, and learning through friends of the better opportunities found here, came to the continent."[27] Third, only seven of the twenty began their tenancies as sharecroppers. Most started as cash tenants. Fourth, thirteen of the twenty were aided by credit from mainly Asian shopkeepers. When they first began, "They were provided with supplies on credit by Chinese dealers in San Jose, by Japanese shopkeepers in San Jose and Alviso, and by a white dealer in Santa Clara."[28] And finally, supplementary employment by both men and women was necessary in most cases:

> Thirteen of these 20, and the wives in several instances, work for wages for from one to four years while developing their farms and berry patches. The men find employment at $1.50 per day on the fruit ranches not far away while the women secure work in the cannery at Alviso, where their earnings, which are on a piece basis, average more than $1 per day. The older farmers can now make a living without taking outside work, but those who have leased land more recently frequently combine work for wages with work on their plots of ground.[29]

Highly revealing of the daily realities of these farm families at Agnew and Alviso is the following description of their homes: "The houses are 'boxed up' of rough boards or 'shakes,' unbattened, unplastered, and not ceiled. In the majority of cases one room serves as living room, kitchen, and dining room, but in some cases a shed–like 'lean-to' is provided for cooking and eating. The floors are uncarpeted and the walls unadorned save for picture advertisements."[30] Such living conditions, noted the report, fell far below the standard of white tenant farmers, reinforcing our contention that Japanese farm tenancy was only a step removed from migrant labor.

Transitions: From Migrant Labor to Tenancy

Japanese farmers in the Santa Clara Valley moved from migrant laborers to tenants in a relatively short period of time. That phenomenon is probably more indicative of the changing social relations of the region than the successful efforts of Japanese migrants to resist impermanence. The changeover from the early American period to the progressive era was accompanied by a transition from large landholdings of grains to smaller tracts of orchards. Asian migrants, Chinese and Japanese, supplied much of the essential labor and political fodder for those changes. The Chinese first arrived in the valley during the period of paternalism and grain farming. Grain farming required comparatively minimal labor. The role of the Chinese in the political economy, accordingly, was primarily that of non-agricultural laborer — railroad worker, land clearer, domestic, and miner. Chinese agricultural labor in the county involved some work as "farm-hands" on the grain ranches, and the cultivation of vegetable gardens to supplement the local diet. Later, during the transition from grains to orchards, the Chinese supplied the crucial labor required in the young orchards and the seed and berry farms.

The Japanese overlapped the Chinese, arriving during the transformation to the orchard phase. Their role in the political economy was both as agricultural laborer and tenant farmer. Thus, the prevailing social relations and the overall pattern of land tenancy evidently helped to determine the nature of the Asian agricultural presence. Large landholdings and industrial agriculture characteristically required migrant labor; smaller parcels and family farms and ranches, on the other hand, were more conducive to share or cash tenancy. Such was the situation in the Santa Clara Valley about the turn of the century.

The Immigration Commission study of the Agnew and Alviso cluster of Japanese farms concluded: "The majority appear to be strongly determined to 'get on,' to purchase land, and to reside permanently in this country." [31] That senti-

ment reveals that the distance between those clusters and the growing Nihonmachi in San Jose during the early 1900s was not simply one of geography. It was also cultural. Nihonmachi was a bachelor society, a migrant labor pool, a place of discontinuity and impermanence. The farm clusters, in contrast, were the beginnings of "real" communities, of families and children, of continuity and tradition. The gap, of course, would diminish over the years, and Nihonmachi would develop into a distinctive community of its own. Still, it seems that the origins of the Japanese American community in the valley were rooted in the farming clusters at Alviso and Agnew. That rootedness, however, was threatened and ultimately stunted by progressive politics and the anti-Japanese movement in the valley.

Harvesting strawberries on NKS farm, c.1905. Nakamura, Kino and Sakauye farmed strawberries from 1900 to 1906. The workers employed by NKS farm made a dollar a day. The trays to hold the berries were made by the Wayne Basket Company in San Jose's Nihonmachi.
Courtesy of Sakauye Family, California History Center Archives.

Yuwakichi Sakauye (l) and friend (r) on wagon loaded with strawberry crates. During harvest time, the NKS farmers competed with fellow Wakayama *ken* farmers at Kino Farm for the fastest pickers, fullest load, and earliest arrival at the Milpitas train depot to meet the 4 p.m. Oakland-bound train. The picture was taken in 1904 or 1905.
Courtesy of Eiichi Sakauye.

Issei pioneer, Yuwakichi Sakauye, picking pears. The Sakauyes were one of the few Japanese orchardists in the valley. Yuwakichi specialized in pears, and his son, Eiichi, continued that interest by grafting and propagating over twenty varieties of pears.
Courtesy of Eiichi Sakauye.

Japanese migrant laborers, pear pickers, on the L. Block Farms in Santa Clara.
Courtesy of California History Center Archives.

Unknown. The photograph, nonetheless, depicts vividly the bachelor society — the large number of men, a solitary Japanese woman and child, and what appears to be a rooming house in the background.
Courtesy of Grant Shimizu.

Japanese workers who farmed
beans on Senter Road, 1913.
Iwamatsu Kawahara, far right,
flanked by his wife and daughter.
*Courtesy of Kawahara Family, California
History Center Archives.*

Funeral in San Jose, probably
during the late 1890s. For the
Japanese in America, especially for
Buddhists, the funeral photograph
was important documentation for
the family in Japan that the
deceased was given a proper
funeral. Note the predominance of
men, and the place where the
photograph was taken, at the
undertaker's (the Buddhist church
was not yet built).

Yamato Bath House on Sixth Street in San Jose Nihon-machi. The owner, Denjiro Hamaguchi, is standing in the doorway. The occasion is New Year's Day 1911. The bath house typified the Japanese migrant labor period. The Yamato Bath House also featured pool tables and rooms for boarders upstairs. Genkichi Minato purchased the bath house in 1919. It was at the time a favorite of people from Wakayama *ken*. Bath hours were from 6-11 p.m. and each bath cost 15¢. Eventually the bath house became known as Minato-Yu.
Courtesy of Kanemoto Collection, California History Center Archives.

Japanese American Branch Office,
San Jose Nihonmachi.

Gathering of the Hiroshima *ken* club in front of a boardinghouse owned by Yamamoto in Nihonmachi, San Jose, c. 1920. The bachelor society was still a reality when this photograph was taken.

Issei women, Mrs. Kimura (l) and Nonoshi Miwa (r), sit for a formal portrait in San Francisco, c. 1907. Issei women, like Issei men, generally adopted Western clothing soon after arriving in the United States.
Courtesy of Joe Y. Akahoshi.

Jizaemon Akahoshi with delivery cart in St. James Park. Akahoshi began his Japanese Laundry in 1906 on E. Santa Clara Street in San Jose. Soon other laundries owned by Japanese immigrants sprang up in other parts of San Jose and in Santa Clara and Saratoga.
Courtesy of Joe Y. Akahoshi.

Footnotes

[1] U.S. Immigration Commission, *Reports: Immigrants in Industries,* XXIV, Government Printing Office: Washington, D.C., 1911, 199.

[2] Immigration Commission, *Reports,* XXIV, 199-201.

[3] Immigration Commission, *Reports,* XXIV, 200.

[4] Immigration Commission, *Reports,* XXIV, 200.

[5] Immigration Commission, *Reports,* XXIV, 208.

[6] Immigration Commission, *Reports,* XXIV, 203.

[7] Oral History, Hisao Omori, November 2, 1983.

[8] Oral History, Yoshio Ando, October 26, 1983.

[9] Oral History, Eiichi Sakauye, April 27, 1983.

[10] Yamato Ichihashi, *Japanese in the United States,* Arno Press: New York, 1969 edition, 174.

[11] Patti Jo N. Hirabayashi, "San Jose Nihonmachi," unpubl. M.A. thesis, San Jose State University, 1977, 8.

[12] Steven Misawa (ed.), *Beginnings: Japanese Americans in San Jose,* San Jose Japanese American Community Senior Service: San Jose, 1981, 12.

[13] *San Jose Mercury,* February 6, 1908.

[14] *San Jose Mercury,* March 20, 1909.

[15] According to court records, Fue Yamashita filed for divorce on April 8, 1908, from her husband, Kutaro Yamashita, case number 17471.

[16] *San Jose Mercury,* August 19, 1908.

[17] *San Jose Mercury,* September 21, 23, 26, 1908.

[18] *San Jose Mercury,* November 8, 1908, December 12, 1908, and March 23, 28, 1909.

[19] See also, *San Jose Mercury,* February 20, 1908.

[20] These included the following families: Ando, Araki, Ezaki, Hayakawa, Kurasaki, and Nakamura.

[21] Oral History, Yoshio Ando, October 26, 1983.

[22] H.S. Foote (ed.), *Pen Pictures From the Garden of the World,* The Lewis Publishing Company: Chicago, 1888, 172-73.

[23] Oral History, Shigio Masunaga, June 13, 15, 1984; and telephone conversation, December 21, 1984.

[24] Oral History, Eiichi Sakauye, April 27, 1983.

[25] Immigration Commission, *Reports,* XXIV, 445-46.

[26] Immigration Commission, *Reports,* XXIV, 446.

[27] Immigration Commission, *Reports,* XXIV, 447.

[28] Immigration Commission, *Reports,* XXIV, 448.

[29] Immigration Commission, *Reports,* XXIV, 448.

[30] Immigration Commission, *Reports,* XXIV, 449.

[31] Immigration Commission, *Reports,* XXIV, 449.

Momo-no-mi
PEACH

CHAPTER 4
PROGRESSIVES AND THE ANTI-JAPANESE MOVEMENT, 1899-1920

The Japanese struggle for a permanent community in the valley was met by newer forms of exploitation by the dominant class. The orchard phase coincided with the period of Japanese migration to the valley and witnessed a change in the community power structure from paternalism to progressivism. The transition was also accompanied by a more sophisticated strategy vis-a-vis the Japanese community for maintaining a cheap Asian labor force.

Politics in the Orchard Phase

The new century seemed to invigorate the progressive movement in the Santa Clara Valley. The canning and fruit-drying operations opened international markets, labor unions were gaining strength, and a large middle class of managers, orchardists, and mercantilists had emerged. These elements felt embarrassed and economically restricted by community leaders like John D. Mackenzie and Southern Pacific lawyer Louis O'Neil who had taken over a reasonably extensive spoils' system, and for a while at least, expanded it.

These practices did not befit the image of a city that was now home to a sophisticated and lucrative agricultural enterprise, and the pressures to render the city more amenable to its new economy could not forever be resisted. The Mackenzie machine and the patronage system, therefore, found itself confronted with formidable opposition — a new generation of progressives re-dedicated to bringing true prosperity to the valley.

Prominent among those progressives were E.A. and J.O. Hayes, attorneys who had gained swift recognition as organizers of local fruit growers' associations.[1] By 1901 the Hayes brothers had purchased both the *San Jose Herald* and the *San Jose Mercury*, which were expeditiously transformed into conduits of progressive propaganda; and by 1905 Everis "Red" Hayes was elected to the U.S. House of Representatives, where he served seven terms.

The progressives gained the support of the local unions that were beginning to rise to prominence, including the carpenters and the typesetters. The union movement, which had theretofore displayed impetuosity and radical tendencies, was beginning to display qualities of legal-rationalism to which the progressives were quite receptive. In an article published in the *San Francisco Labor Clarion*, Samuel Gompers praised Red Hayes as an "indefatigable" friend of labor.[2] Of course, this does not mean that the progressives lent their support to the embryonic cannery and field workers organizations, or to the Toilers of the World, a union that in 1917 struck at seven of San Jose's largest canning operations. Comprised mostly of Italians, many of them women, this unskilled labor union was branded by the Hayes newspapers as an uncontrollable ally of the Communist Party. Instead, it was the American Federation of Labor, already an established and staid bureaucracy, that appealed to the progressives, and local progressives like Hayes and state senator Herbert Jones[3] came to be known as strong, albeit limited, union supporters.

This reveals an important characteristic of the

local progressives — that although the leadership was decidedly professional and middle class, it was clear, in San Jose at least, that the real aim of the progressives was not so much economic predominance as it was social homogeneity, not so much the limitation of interests as a limitation on how interests were to be pursued. Of course this is not an indication of altruism, for the standard of the homogeneity was clearly middle class Protestant, and the proper mode of pursuing interests was legal-rational — which clearly favored the well-educated progressives who were at a real disadvantage under the patronage ("patriarchal") system that preceded them.[4] It does, however, explain why the progressives were so friendly to the skilled labor unions; for the economic concessions were perceived as a minor inconvenience to an alliance with "true Americans."

Similarly, it is clear why, despite an appreciation of their economic contribution, the progressives were repelled by the unskilled Italian labor groups, and even more by the Japanese. E.A. Hayes, who made the first ever anti-Japanese speech in the House of Representatives (December 1905), repeatedly emphasized his concern with the Japanese inability to assimilate rather than their economic threat: ". . .if the Japanese are a menace to the peace and progress of the Pacific Coast in a competitive sense. . .as a menace they should be very much more feared in a racial sense. . .there is no common association nor can there be between the yellow and white races."[5]

"Progress" in the Anti-Japanese Movement

The problem for the new leaders was to continue the rhetoric for homogeneity while simultaneously retaining the essential economic contribution of Japanese labor — and at the same time to avoid the label of "Asian lover," as J.J. Owen before them was unable to do. The progressives' apparent ambivalence toward the Japanese, engendered by the paradoxical adherence to economic progress and racial homogeneity, allowed a strategy that was more calculated than impetuous, and more instrumental than venal, than the anti-Chinese activity of the prior era. There is a good deal of evidence, both at the state and local level, that the progressives' opposition to the Japanese was as much a response to non-progressive politicians as it was an overwhelming fear of the Japanese presence. Thus, policies and attitudes exerted on the Japanese were much different, perhaps even more insidious, than the blatancies of the anti-Chinese period.

That the progressives adopted anti-Japanese positions to avoid accusations of un-Americanism like those suffered by J.J. Owen can be shown in communications from the highest levels of the progressive movement. When President Woodrow Wilson, representing the party that had for so long tormented the progressives with racist demagoguery, appealed to Governor Hiram Johnson and his progressive colleagues in California to moderate their anti-Japanese statements in light of the impending, and potentially lucrative, Panama Pacific International Exposition, Johnson was tickled at the opportunity to turn the tables. Thus, at the expense of the Japanese, Johnson rejected the supplication and pursued anti-Japanese legislation with the purpose of embarrassing Wilson, William Jennings Bryan (Wilson's Secretary of State, who had come to California to press for moderation),[6] and the Democratic Party. In a letter to Chester Rowell, Governor Johnson anticipated Wilson's gestures and gloated:

> The situation is unique and interesting now, and not only interesting, but one out of which we can get a good deal of satisfaction.... I think before the session adjourns the present administration may be asking us, in exactly the same fashion as previous administrations have asked us, to take no position.[7]

As far as the Santa Clara Valley is concerned, we have already mentioned the local representative of past innocence, J.J. Owen, and the price he had to pay for merely ambivalent attitudes. Thus, there was clearly a local inspiration for the cautious and vengeful attitudes of Hiram Johnson and we would expect second-generation progressives in the valley to be much more careful about revealing their own ambivalent sympathies, even if they were based solely on a recognition of the value of exploitation. This helps to explain why the progressives' ideal was for homogeneity, and the thought of a large and permanent Japanese community upset their vision.

This does not mean, however, that there were not elements of true revulsion in the progressives' attitude toward the Japanese. Rather, the revulsion seemed to be more compartmentalized than the prior Chinese hatred, and was aimed at repelling the possibility of a heterogeneous, multi-ethnic community. The progressives, including those from the Santa Clara Valley, had waged what they saw as an uphill battle against what they felt were representatives of one inferior ethnicity (Irish Catholics), and they certainly did not want to surrender their growing predominance to another. Leading progressives like Chester Rowell envisioned an alliance between the old aristocracy and their Asian co-conspirators leading to a resurgence of a "feudal plutocracy of white and brown aristocrats and brown and black common people."[8] James Phelan, whose anti-Japanese attitudes drove him to distraction, also spoke of the threat:

> In the presence of the Japanese you will find one of the principal reasons of our economic and social disturbances. Let us diplomatically say that we regard the non-assimilable Japanese as efficient human machines, but as such, they are a menace to our prosperity and happiness. Then the more sensitive citizens of Japan may find some consolation in our confession of economic inferiority.[9]

Clearly, then, it was the Japanese economic contribution that led to the fears of this social intrusion. But just as clearly, it would be the best of both progressive worlds if the economic contribution of the Japanese could be maintained within a political and social climate that rendered assimilation and fair competition impossible. Residential segregation — the Chinatown and Nihonmachi ghettoes — and discrimination in employment, in effect, a dual labor market — helped to ensure the desired distance. Above all, perhaps, the alien land laws, especially as they were implemented in the Santa Clara Valley, made the ideal possible.

Alien Land Laws and the "Best of Both Worlds"

A number of local phenomena apparently led to the conclusion that the land laws were used to intimidate the Japanese in the valley rather than exclude them, to reap their economic contribution without rewarding it with the liberal ideal of opportunity. The first phenomenon is that as far as we could determine, there was never an official prosecution of the land laws in the valley; indeed, there was very little official interest in them once they were passed. In fact, in 1921, Santa Clara Valley resident and landlord of a number of Japanese farmers, J.J. O'Brien, sued in the district court of northern California to enjoin state Attorney General U.S. Webb from enforcing the 1920 Alien Land Law. O'Brien owned ten acres on the Coleman Younger tract in the county, and wanted to enter a sharecropping agreement with Issei farmer, J. Inouye. The court ruled in favor of O'Brien, but on appeal to the state supreme court, the justices ruled that the law forbade Issei (aliens ineligible for citizenship) from sharecropping.[10]

The second phenomenon that contributes to the "best of both worlds" conclusion is that after the passage of the 1920 Alien Land Law the concern over the Japanese in the valley, especially that coming from Hayes' *San Jose Mercury,* seemed virtually to disappear. Although a few groups continued to press for complete exclusion and even expulsion, the Santa Clara Valley seemed content merely to ignore the Chinese and Japanese communities. There were no burnings as in the anti-Chinese period, and there were few attempts to mobilize boycotts. The progressives seemed to have reached the perfect balance: the Japanese were allowed to make crucial agricultural contributions to the valley, but were not allowed access to the white community, to the white economy, or even the white school system.[11] Further, Japanese farmers felt constrained by the alien land laws and the mere threat of their enforcement. The progressives, thus, had successfully achieved what had eluded Owen — a decidedly anti-Japanese stance while reaping benefits from the Japanese presence.

The Bayside Cannery

Perhaps the best proof, that anti-Asian activities during the period of progressive dominance were more instrumental than thorough, was the flourishing of a cannery operated completely by local Chinese in the midst of anti-Asian activities. The very existence of the Bayside Cannery demonstrates the "selectivity" of anti-Asianism in the area. We believe that since the Chinese were no longer the preferred source of cheap farm labor, and since their numbers had dwindled significantly in the valley after the various assaults on San Jose's Chinatown, the Bayside enterprise was allowed to function in benign neglect. This testifies to a more contrived and purposeful era of anti-Asian activity, directed only against the specific minority that could provide the necessary field labor at "acceptable" wage levels.

The 1906 earthquake destroyed the small and struggling Precita Canning Company that had been organized in 1890 by Sai Yin Chew, an immigrant from the Toishan district of China.[12] Seeking a more lucrative location, the Chew family rebuilt in the town of Alviso and renamed the operation the

Bayside Canning Company.

In 1906, Sai Yin's son, Tom Foon, entered the business. It was Tom Foon who, by expanding the business beyond tomato canning and investing in the newest and most advanced equipment, was able to promote the cannery to a major industrial concern in the valley. By 1924, Tom Foon had acquired two other plants, at Isleton and Mayfair, and was packing 600,000 cases of fruits and vegetables and grossing over $3 million per year.

Along with the canneries, Tom Foon was able to purchase and lease farmland throughout northern California under the name of the Tom Foon Ranch Company. The Company held 8,000 acres on Twitchel Island and other islands in the Delta region, 180 acres near Yuba City planted in peaches, and several hundred acres near Dos Palos planted in rice. Tom Foon's granddaughter claims that at one time, Tom Foon leased an estimated 80,000 acres throughout the Santa Clara and San Joaquin Valleys, thus providing suitable and accessible produce for the Bayside canning activity. Several Japanese farmers were so employed on Tom Foon's orchards in the Santa Clara Valley.[13] His corporation also leased land from valley landowners including Santa Clara County (a practice that would have hardly been condoned in the earlier era of anti-Chinese hysteria), with the stipulation that he leave it cleared, and thus ready for development or more lucratuve leases.[14] Tom Foon also provided mortgages to small landowners, including Japanese, in return for cash or a part of the crop.[15]

As for capital, which was often scarce particularly among the canneries, Tom Foon was fortunate to have married into a wealthy family — and Lee G. Ching and her family invested heavily in the Bayside venture. In addition, Tom Foon belonged to the Bing Kong Tong, and had relatives in the Shew Hing Association, both of which provided Chinese investment capital. It is clear, however, that Tom Foon Chew would not have expanded and prospered had he not been supported by the Caucasian community and its bankers.

Tom Foon became close friends with A.P. Gianinni, founder of Bank of America, and his Alviso operation was financed by a number of the local banks. Newspaper articles on Tom Foon invariably praised how in speech, dress, and mannerism he so closely resembled an "American."[16] Having been denied admittance into the San Francisco chapter of the Scottish Rites, he was later honored as a member of the San Jose temple with the thirty-third degree — rare for an Anglo, much less for an Asian.

Tom Foon's son, Charlie Chew, was not as competent as his father, nor did he have a personality that endeared him to the Anglo community, so following the death of Tom Foon in 1931, the Bayside Canning Company faded into oblivion. The company went into receivership and the assets were sold to cover the debts that were no longer being extended by the white banks. Nevertheless, for about twenty years a cannery owned and operated by a Chinese American flourished in the Santa Clara Valley.

The success of the Bayside Cannery, which demonstrated a "selective" anti-Asian posture, along with the less than stringent application of the land laws and a marked reduction in blatant acts of harassment, is indicative of the development of a sophisticated form of racism. In this type of political climate, community leaders were able to maintain an atmosphere of fear and vulnerability among the Japanese community without invoking sheer terror and exile, as had been the case earlier with the Chinese community.

The Anti-Japanese Movement and Public Opinion

The complexity of the anti-Japanese movement in the Santa Clara Valley during the period of dependency and progressive politics can be traced in the shifts in the newspaper coverage of that ethnic minority. Those changes in editorial positions and news accounts reflect the development of a sophisticated form of racism, and parallel the transition that the Japanese underwent in the valley — from migrant labor to dependent community. Although we recognize that newspaper coverage and public opinion are not one and the same, we believe that the press frequently helps to shape public opinion and functions to sustain the status quo.

During the period of Japanese migrant labor, from about 1895 to 1907, Japanese workers were welcomed and were portrayed as distinctive from Chinese laborers. In an editorial on November 23, 1901, the *Mercury* directed the following diatribe against Santa Clara Valley representatives to the Chinese Exclusion League Convention held two days earlier. "The promoters of an extension of the Chinese law will be wise if they do not try to have its provisions apply to the Japanese." That same theme was reiterated in a *Mercury* editorial on January 18, 1905, in which Japanese migrants were differentiated from Chinese laborers, and even bestowed with admirable European-like traits.

We quote in full:

In some quarters a question as to the necessity for the regulation of Japanese immigration into the United States has arisen. A law after the manner of the Chinese exclusion act has been suggested, according to the *New York Commercial Journal.* While the Pacific coast States believe that the exclusion of Chinese has saved them from incomparable economical and industrial woes, there is hardly any likelihood of the necessity arising for the consideration of similar laws in relation to the Japanese. Those Japanese immigrants whom we have admitted have proved very good citizens — exceptionally good for the most part — and there has been talk of establishing colonies of them in the rice growing States along the Gulf of Mexico. This scheme is retarded or has been abandoned through the reluctance of the Japanese themselves.

For the next few years, even if an end were to come speedily to the war, the Japanese will have all they can do to develop their own country, and there will be comparatively little immigration to any other. In any event it is not at all likely that sufficent [sic] numbers would set their faces in this direction to mar our occidental institutions or to interfere with the welfare of our laboring classes, which became direct sufferers through the influx of Chinese in the years prior to the enactment of the exclusion laws. In our consideration of the chief Asiatic races, moreover, we are learning to dissociate the Chinese and the Japanese — and to the later [sic] we now attribute many

of the national characteristics that the
European nations admire and possess.

Beginning in the fall of 1906, however, the
Mercury reversed itself and began a steady barrage
of anti-Japanese news coverage and editorials.
Congressman E.A. Hayes led the assault as
recorded in the pages of the *Mercury*. On
September 17, 1906, he reportedly addressed the
meeting of the Japanese Exclusion League in San
Francisco and said, "If we are to have war with
Japan, let's have it right away. We're ready and they
are not." He repeated his anti-Japanese sentiment at
a Republican Party rally in Saratoga in October.
Later that month at a meeting in San Francisco, he
spoke once again in favor of Japanese exclusion.[17]
In December, the San Jose Chamber of Commerce
launched "a gigantic advertising scheme" to bring
5,000 white families to the Santa Clara Valley, and
in that way avoid the need for Japanese migrant
laborers, hundreds of "yellow skinned pickers," by
substituting in their place the children of those
white immigrants.[18]

On Sunday morning, September 1, 1907, valley
residents read the following in the agricultural
section of the *Mercury* under the prominent by-line,
"Dear Little Brown Men: How They Do Things
to White Folks When They Get the Power":

It is announced that when the vineyardists
of San Joaquin county got ready to employ
grape-pickers they found the little brown men
all ready for them and were compelled to pay
$2.50 per day or let their grapes rot on the
vines. What one Jap said all Japs said, and
there was no help to be had. And the grape-

growers took their medicine. If the weather is
favorable the growers this year will probably
have a little money left after paying their help.
If rains come and extra trimming is required
they will lose money. Either way is perfectly
satisfactory to the Japs. It will be $2.50 a day
just the same.

We repeat the warning which we have
frequently given, that if the Japanese coolies
are allowed to get a monopoly of the work
the employers will not be permitted to make a
single dollar. The Japs will take the land.
When a vineyardist discovers that life at the
mercy of the Japs is not worth living he leases
his vineyard to one of them and this is the
beginning of the end of that district as a white
man's country.

Later that same month, in the September 21,
1907, issue of the *Mercury*, the images of the Chinese
and Japanese were reversed. The Chinese were now
portrayed as "respectable citizens" while the
Japanese, in comparison, constituted a "serious
menace":

San Jose's workingmen, householders and
small dealers are observing with alarm the
steady inflow of Japanese into Santa Clara
county, and especially the growing population
of the little brown men in this city. The sons
of the Mikado are the yellow perils of San
Jose. John Chinaman, once believed to be the
greatest menace that confronted the future of
the Pacific coast, has become, by contrast with
his Mongolian neighbors, quite a respectable
citizen. The Chinaman is content to earn his

living as a laborer, a cook, and is seldom in competition with white merchants.... The Chinaman is a pioneer in California, but he has never presumed to dare the wrath of the whites as the later-arriving Jap is now doing.

The "Japanese problem," the article continued, was the settlement of Japanese in the valley. Walter Page, secretary of the Japanese-Korean Exclusion League, was quoted as saying, "That the Japs are settling here in ever-increasing numbers is an appalling fact; in fact, it is computed that their local community has increased over 500 percent in seven years. And they have only just begun to arrive, comparatively speaking." The fear, thus, was the growing clusters of Japanese farms and the developing Nihonmachi in San Jose. The Japanese were no longer transitory groups of migrant men, blankets over their shoulders; they were becoming a settled community. The prospect of permanence was frightening.

Yet to the elites, the brokers of community power, permanent settlements of Japanese farmers offered another opportunity for profits. These farmers could continue to toil in the fields and orchards of the valley, not as migrants but as tenants. Apparently, even the notorious anti-Asianist James D. Phelan, mayor of San Francisco and later U.S. Senator from California, profited from Japanese tenancy in the valley. From 1917 to 1919, Kotaro and Fude Omori share-cropped tomatoes with Edward Lane in the vicinity of Kelly Park in San Jose. The relationship was not extraordinary except that Edward Lane in turn leased the property from none other than J.D. Phelan. During that period, two other Japanese families sharecropped on that same tract of land.[19]

That simple story sheds considerable light on the intricacies of the anti-Japanese movement since 1907. Senator Phelan, at least in this instance, embodied the dichotomy between rhetoric on one hand and pragmatic gains on the other. Exclusionists during the progressive period might have protested loudly against the Japanese "invasion," but many stood to gain from their presence. Their public posturing might have threatened expulsion, yet their implementations were to the contrary. The welcome mat placed at the landing at Alviso during the period of Japanese migrant labor was unceremoniously withdrawn when the Japanese formed permanent communities. All the while, of course, the valley's landowners profited from Japanese workers.

The following period, that of dependency, necessitated new tactics. The balance arrived at resulted in "the best of both worlds" for the progressives. Not only was the "Japanese issue" indispensible during elections it served a specific function in maintaining Japanese dependency. Its purpose in helping to shape public opinion was analogous to the alien land laws.[20] It was not designed to drive the Japanese from the valley like the Chinese before them; such blatancies were of a lower order. Rather, it served to segregate the Japanese from the mainstream, render them politically impotent, and restrict their economic advance.

Footnotes

[1] See Robert Couchman, *The Sunsweet Story,* Sunsweet Growers: San Jose, 1967.

[2] *Labor Clarion,* August 30, 1912. The October 22 issue of the *Union,* the labor organ of Santa Clara County, also praised Hayes for his favorable voting record.

[3] Jones's support for the established unions, and concomitant neglect of less organized workers can be seen in his attitudes toward exemptions from labor laws for unskilled workers, and his progressive stands vis-a-vis the trades. See his Papers in the Green Library, Rare Book Room, Stanford University.

[4] An excellent description of the respective attributes of patriarchal and legal-rational organizations is in, James Q. Wilson, *Political Organizations,* Basic Books: New York, 1972.

[5] *San Jose Mercury Herald,* January 8, 1920.

[6] Handwritten notes of the meetings conducted by Bryan can be found in the Jones Papers, Green Library.

[7] Hiram Johnson to Chester Rowell, March 17, 1913. Rowell Manuscripts, Bancroft Library, University of California, Berkeley.

[8] Chester Rowell to Payson J. Treat, May 3, 1913. Rowell Manuscripts, Bancroft Library, University of California, Berkeley.

[9] *San Francisco Examiner,* April 30, 1913. These kinds of sentiments continued into the period of agitation which led to the 1920 legislation. On June 17, 1920, Robert Newton Lynch, vice-president and manager of the California Trades and Development Board spoke to the San Jose Chamber of Commerce, and claimed that "the Japanese are a forceful, dominant people" and "there must be legislation which thoroughly prevents them from getting into the country in such numbers to dominate any portion of it." *San Jose Mercury Herald,* June 18, 1920.

[10] Frank F. Chuman, *The Bamboo People: The Law and Japanese-Americans,* Publisher's Inc.: Del Mar, CA, 1976, 86-87; and Emil T.H. Bunje, *The Story of Japanese Farming in California,* University of California, Berkeley, 1937, 107-13.

[11] Santa Clara County was able to sidestep the whole issue of segregation within school districts by establishing the Orchard School District, which still exists today. It consists of one elementary school, and before World War II it catered wholly to Japanese American children.

[12] Much of the information in this section was obtained in an interview with Sylvia Sue Minnick, granddaughter of Tom Foon Chew, on June 5, 1984. The authors would also like to thank Mayo Ryan for his help in researching the Bayside Cannery.

[13] Wilma Tognazzini, "Pioneers in California," unpubl. manuscript, San Jose Historical Museum Archives; and Oral History, Sylvia Sue Minnick, June 5, 1984.

[14] See, for instance, deed filing number C-21669 of November 21, 1924, Recorder's Office, Santa Clara County.

[15] See, for instance, Santa Clara County Mortgage Records, 1922, 69. T. Iwagaki mortgaged a number of vehicles to Tom Foon for $2,500 on December 7, 1922.

[16] See especially his obituary in the *San Jose Mercury,* February 25, 1931.

[17] *San Jose Mercury,* October 9, 1906, and October 24, 1906.

[18] *San Jose Mercury,* December 6, 1906.

[19] Oral History, Hisao Omori, November 2, 1983.

[20] For newspaper and contemporary surveys undertaken in Santa Clara County, see, Ruth Miriam Fowler, "Some Aspects of Public Opinion Concerning the Japanese in Santa Clara County," unpubl. M.A. thesis, Stanford University, 1934; and Charles N. Reynolds, "Oriental-White Race Relations in Santa Clara County, California," unpubl. Ph.D. dissertation, Stanford University, 1927.

Hanabishi
CALIFORNIA POPPY

CHAPTER 5
JAPANESE DEPENDENCY, 1907-1942

Clusters of Japanese farms appeared along the fertile crescent extending from Milpitas and Berryessa to the east and Mayfair and Santa Clara to the west. If Alviso and Agnew marked the embryonic beginnings of a Japanese American community in the valley, the fertile soils of the lowland crescent comprised its womb. It was not as if the area was all that desirable. Like the pattern established elsewhere in California, Asians were generally relegated to places that were not preferred by the earlier-arriving whites. Flooding was a common occurrence in the crescent. Refuse from San Jose and the valley's hinterland drained toward the bay and collected along the crescent's shore. Saltwater from the bay sometimes seeped into the freshwater table killing the crops. Despite those natural disadvantages, Japanese farmers planted their gardens and the crops took root.

The most fundamental distinction, of course, that separates migrant labor from dependency is that the former denotes a temporary presence, while the latter denotes a permanent one. Those conditions, whether as sojourners or settlers, were not un-connected from the wider political economy, nor were they entirely the result of Japanese preference. They were the products of the struggle between oppression and resistance.

Women and Work

Without doubt, the foremost factor in the development of permanent communities was the immigration of Japanese women. While "picture brides" might have been pivotal in increasing the number of Japanese women in America, the situation in the Santa Clara Valley was somewhat different. Our oral history survey reinforces the findings of the 1908 Immigration Commission study of Japanese farmers at Alviso and Agnew. A clear majority were already married when they arrived in the valley, and women were conspicuously present in the earliest Japanese settlements in the Santa Clara Valley.

These women comprised sources of labor that increased the productivity of the household unit. As noted in the 1908 study, most of the Japanese farms in Alviso and Agnew were able to survive, especially during the first few years, through the combined efforts of both husband and wife on the family farm and outside through wage labor. In fact, households frequently made decisions in employment based on utilizing the labor of all of its members, and in that way, maximized the productivity of the unit. For example, while John Hayakawa was employed as a pruner and tractor driver on the Sweetbriar Orchards, his elderly parents and wife intercropped cucumbers between the rows of young trees. Landowners also benefited from that kind of full employment. Kaso Hayakawa, John's father, worked in 1925 on the Kenneth Miner ranch in Cupertino. After about eighteen months laboring in the orchard, Kaso was dismissed by Miner and replaced with a Mr. Sato. Sato offered to assume Kaso's tasks but offered a sharecropping proposal for strawberries to be grown on four vacant acres of the ranch, managed by his wife and children.[1]

More directly, women have been credited with the transition to settled communities because of their reproductive powers. This point is clearly significant. The children, born in America, were citizens and, when of age, acquired the franchise and the ability to own real property. They attended the public schools, acculturated, and held little national attachment to Japan. The Nisei, thus, served to secure the family more firmly to America. In one instance, the fates of the children quite literally led to permanent residence in the valley. Shigekichi Kawashima left Fukuoka for the sugar plantations of Hawaii when he was about seventeen years old. He later moved to San Francisco, and eventually found his way to Nebraska. In 1927, Shigekichi outfitted a one-ton Chevrolet truck in camper-like fashion and headed west for California en route to Japan. The children, however, contracted chickenpox, the journey was delayed, and the family unpacked in Alviso. The stay became permanent.[2]

Women's reproductive abilities aside, their labor should not be undervalued. Ichihashi, for instance, reported that the dues paid by women to join the "clubs" around which labor gangs were organized were the same as paid by men because women were considered equals as wage-earners. Describing the Japanese "clubs" in Watsonville, Ichihashi wrote: "Another interesting fact is that out of 640 members, a little less than 150 are women. These women, of course, are all married and with their husbands. The wives join the club because the membership of their husbands will not entitle them to the club benefits, the ground being that she can earn as much as her husband."[3] Also, while work

tasks were generally divided on the basis of gender, Japanese men and women apparently received equal pay for equal work.[4]

Cost of Labor

Another factor in the transition from migrant labor to dependent community was the rise in the cost of Japanese labor. The Immigration Commission cited an example in which an almost exclusive reliance on Japanese labor by Santa Clara Valley prune growers led to higher wages for those workers. An added explanation for those higher wages might be the Japanese drive for self-sufficiency:

In one or two exceptional cases. . .Japanese harvest laborers have been paid more than white help. One instance of this was during the prune harvest in the Santa Clara Valley in 1910, when Japanese were paid $2 per day. This resulted from the dependence of this industry for years upon Japanese labor, so that the scarcity of Japanese workers in 1910 enabled those present to demand much higher wages than formerly, and the growers were not prepared to meet the demands by bringing in white labor to compete with the Japanese, and white men did not seek this work voluntarily as the growers had been employing Japanese almost exclusively for years.[5]

That in turn led the landowners to seek cheaper sources of labor. During the 1920s and 1930s, Filipino and Mexican migrants filled that need, and during the Great Depression poor whites added to the widening pool of exploitable labor.

Exclusionism and Dependency

The immigration of Japanese women and the struggle for higher wages can be viewed as a form of resistance. Conversely, the movement of Japanese workers into farm tenancy was not progress pure and simple, nor was that transition due entirely to Japanese resistance. The transformation was to some extent permitted, not gained through toil and conquest. The social relations endemic to Japanese farm tenancy in the valley were more sophisticated than the relations governing migrant labor, and their complexity was in accord with the solution achieved by the dominant class and the progressives.

While the persistence of the Japanese presence in the valley posed a problem to cultural homogeneity, that same reality offered opportunities for economic profit. Thus counterposed were rhetoric and pragmatic gains, white supremacy and Japanese underdevelopment. In the *Mercury's* editorial of March 7, 1907, the paper urged "a calm view" on the Japanese immigration question, reflecting the pragmatic gains realized through Japanese labor:

> We have the utmost confidence in the wisdom and justice of American public opinion, when once it fairly settles on any measure of public policy. That public opinion we wish to win, and this we believe we can do by fairly, fully, earnestly and in good temper, presenting our case. In this way the *Mercury* has tried to treat the matter from the first, and this policy we mean to continue. We commend it to our contemporaries. It may take some time, but we are firmly convinced that the time is not far away when the main contention of our people here in regard to this [Japanese] question will be heartily acquiesced in by the American people. But we cannot win our case by loud and threatening talk in a police court. We shall win it on its merits, by fair trial in the great court of American public opinion.

Public opinion was won over, and it functioned to constrain Japanese self-determination. The latitudes were narrowly defined in segregated residential communities, in the schools for their children, in the places where they conducted business, and in their pattern of employment. Reverend Minoru (Francis) Hayashi, minister of the Wesley United Methodist Church in San Jose's Nihonmachi from 1953 to 1966, recalled the 1920s when he was a student at Stanford University. "Most of the Nisei from Stanford at that time couldn't get the job [sic] in the United States, so they went to Japan. So many Stanford graduates went back to Japan — all different majors. I finished Engineering in 1926, [but] I couldn't get a job, so my parents helped me open an electrical appliance store in San Francisco."[6]

The Alien Land Laws and Dependency

For Japanese farmers, the alien land laws operated in a way similar to public opinion. The laws were designed to limit the farmers' economic advance and to bind them to the prevailing social relations. At the same time, they were politically irresistible to the framers of public policy: they were popular. The 1920 Alien Land Law, an initiative on the state ballot, was passed in Santa Clara County by a margin of 18,635 to 7,862. Senator James D. Phelan and Representative Everis A. Hayes actively campaigned for the initiative both nationally and locally. Hayes, speaking before the San Jose Rotary Club, declared:

> These yellow peoples...have nothing in common with the people of this country.... Should they be free to come to the Pacific shores without restrictions numerically, it would only be a few years when the Americanism now in California would be completely submerged and Japanese ideals and practices would dominate the entire state. Let these people acquire vast tracts of land, which they are doing in spite of the Alien Land Law, and ambitious white Americans will be driven from their land.[7]

In an editorial on January 14, 1920, the *Mercury* echoed the "yellow peril" theme and added the warning that the situation in Hawaii portended what could happen in California. ".... In a very short time the state may be overrun by the peoples of the yellow races; and, as in the case in the Hawaiian Islands, the white population will be in the humiliating position of having a limited authority both in the direction of industries and agricultural matters."

Despite those bald exclusionist sentiments, advocates of the 1920 Alien Land Law were not proposing the complete eradication of Asians in America, nor were they suggesting the expulsion of

Asians from the factories in the field. Instead, their goal was to ensure Asian labor, either migrant or tenant. For instance, V.S. McClatchy, virulent anti-Asianist and newspaper publisher, in 1919 proposed six remedies to the "Japanese problem." These were: cancellation of the Gentlemen's Agreement, exclusion of "picture brides," exclusion of Japanese, forever barring Asians from American citizenship, amending the Constitution to provide that children of aliens ineligible for citizenship be likewise barred from citizenship, and permitting the entrance of Chinese laborers for a fixed term of years for work on specific jobs and returning them to China when they were no longer needed.[8] McClatchy's plan makes clear his underlying purpose and that of the dominant class in the anti-Asian movement — economic gain through Asian migrant labor and dependency.

Thus, in Santa Clara County, public opinion was directed against the Japanese; progressive politicians railed against the yellow "invasion"; the 1920 Alien Land Law passed in a landslide; and, at the same time, prosecution against violators of the law was virtually nonexistent. Moreover, it seems that the Santa Clara County superior court judge during the 1920s was less likely to rule against the Japanese in alien land law cases.[9] The apparently contradictory behavior on the part of the dominant class was not self-negating. Rather, the alien land laws were a "convenient club" held over the heads of Japanese farmers. While seeking to evade the laws, Japanese farmers were acutely aware that the unconventional arrangements arrived at placed them in dire jeopardy. Like undocumented workers, they were subject to easy exploitation on the mere threat that they would be punished. Thus, like public opinion, the laws functioned to maintain Japanese dependency. Recalled San Jose businessman I.K. Ishimatsu:

> I don't go so far as to say the alien land laws threatened our livelihood. But if you wanted to lease or own the land for any purpose, you had to use your children's name and if you didn't have your own children, you would have to take a risk and ask someone who was a citizen and hope everything worked out. A set of books had to be kept up for inspection by the state authorities in order to prove that you were an employee working for a wage. This caused an uneasy feeling because I was informed at the time that the punishment for alien land law violation was condemnation of all the subject's property and imprisonment.[10]

The Pattern of Land Tenure under Dependency

Because of the alien land laws, certain patterns of land tenure emerged among the Japanese farming community in the valley during the period of dependency. Unconventional tenures were commonplace. These included formation of Japanese farm corporations to evade the 1913 Alien Land Law, the use of Nisei intermediaries following 1920, and the development of quasi-sharecropping agreements after 1923. The farm corporations enabled Issei, subject to the restrictions of the 1913 Alien Land Law, to own and lease land through corporations in which they held a majority of the stock. The U.S. House Committee on Immigration

and Naturalization reported the following information on farm corporations in Santa Clara County in 1921:

Name and Place	Capital Stock	Acreage
Antoku Farming Co., Mountain View	$ 5,000	5
Almaden Nashion Farm, San Jose	$20,000	10
Glen Hill Farming Co., San Jose	$10,000	14.75
Harry Farm Co., Mountain View	$10,000	11
Haruta Shinks Farm Co., Sunnyvale	$10,000	30
Kiyomura Farm Co., Mountain View	$ 5,000	3.75
Lincoln Orchard Co., San Jose	$10,000	15.09
McClaughlin Avenue Co., San Jose	$10,000	17
Sugishita Sons Farming Co., San Jose	$ 4,000	5
Tanase Farm Co., Campbell	$10,000	8.09

Table 4. Japanese Farm Corporations, Capital Stock, and Acreage, Santa Clara County, 1921.[11]

The 1920 Alien Land Law closed the loopholes that permitted the farm corporations and the practice of placing land titles under the names of minor children. Accordingly after 1920, Japanese farmers in the valley relied on adult Nisei intermediaries to act as landlords or as guardians. Eiichi Sakauye described how the system operated. Several large landowners in the valley rented parcels to Nisei. These included the Brandt and Cropley ranches in Berryessa, the Able, Bassett, and Curtner ranches in Milpitas, and the Bracher, Brown, Jameson, and Wilcox ranches in Santa Clara.[12] The Nisei in turn subdivided the land for individual Issei farmers who generally occupied the parcels as share-croppers. Each farm was identified by ranch or Nisei landlord name and numbers — for example, Able Camp 1, 2, etc., or (Harry) Hashimoto or (Russell) Hinaga Camp on Trimble Road.[13] The McGinty ranch in Berryessa during the 1930s, thus, held about ten Japanese farming families. The cluster was known as JUF, or Jim Uyeda Farm, after the Nisei landlord who leased about thirty acres on the McGinty property. The farms were numbered JUF 1 through 10. Just adjacent was the Brandt ranch, which held ten additional Japanese families. Uyeda bore the responsibility for the farms in his camp. He helped to arbitrate disputes among his tenants, and encouraged farm productivity.[14]

Profits from Dependency

Despite the provisions of the 1920 Alien Land Law, certain white landowners continued to rent land to Issei farmers. J.J. O'Brien, for instance, had thirty-five Japanese families on his property on Brokaw Road, farms 1 through 35. Katsusaburo Kawahara moved to O'Brien's tract in 1921. He, along with other farmers like the Inouyes, paid cash rent to O'Brien, at $40 per acre plus what was called a "silent commission" of five percent of the gross sales.[15] O'Brien also had Japanese sharecroppers on his land. These farmers sent their produce to the commission houses in San Francisco under the name of O'Brien, ostensibly to maintain the fiction that they were mere laborers. The commission houses sent the checks for the sale of the produce to O'Brien, who in turn deducted his share, normally fifty percent, and a "commission" of five to seven percent of the total for having handled the sale.[16] We can only speculate on whether O'Brien reported to his Japanese wards the exact proceeds received from the sale. Since the payments went directly to O'Brien and prices fluctuated daily, the Japanese had no way of checking on the actual amount received. In another instance concerning a different landlord, Shoji Takeda recalled abuse of the dependent position of Japanese sharecroppers.

> Tomiju Takeda, my father, would produce a beautiful crop, but the owner would receive the total compensation from the buyer and without his knowledge the owner would spend all the money. . . . One particular incident which was told by my father, related the fact, that the owner had spent my father's share of the income and this led to the owner presenting my father with a Jersey cow as his payment.[17]

With those incentives, there is little wonder that O'Brien instituted the suit against state Attorney General Webb to prohibit him from enforcing the 1920 Alien Land Law; there were considerable profits to be made.[18]

Other gains for white landowners included the

racial rent premium. In 1910, there was a broad difference in the average rents received from Japanese and white tenants — $23.29 and $8.95 per acre, respectively. Less measurable but just as real were the improvements made by Japanese farmers on vacant land or on orchards, through inter-cropping by which Japanese tenants were permitted to plant their vegetables between the rows of the landlord's fruit trees. The young orchard trees prospered under that kind of care, leading white orchardists to seek out Japanese tenants.[19] Inter-cropping was especially attractive to orchardists who had little vacant land because it did not require additional space beyond the existing orchard. Furthermore, once the trees had matured, the Japanese tenants could be moved to another area of the property to help develop newly planted trees under the staggered rotation plan.

On vacant land, Japanese farmers enhanced the value of the property by converting what was usually pasture or hilly ground into productive, level gardens. The entire process, requiring immense amounts of labor, took several years to accomplish and was undertaken in step-by-step phases. Many Japanese farmers recognized this and negotiated terms accordingly. Some managed to reduce the rents for opening up new land, while others obtained rights to use the landowner's farm equipment. Still others were able to delay payment on the rent — in effect, a credit arrangement — from monthly to every six months. Such terms were in fact necessary because newly opened land was not all that productive for the first three or four years.[20] That reality brings into sharp focus the exploitive provision of the 1913 Alien Land Law, which permitted Issei cash tenancy for periods of up to three years. At the very point of real productivity, the Issei tenant was susceptible to eviction.

Japanese Underdevelopment

The white landowners' profits were gained at the expense of Japanese underdevelopment. The pattern of Japanese farm tenancy in the valley confirms that contention. Between 1900 and 1942, like the profile established statewide, the progress of Japanese tenants to the ranks of growers showed little change. In 1912, Japanese owned 4 farms in the county totaling some 90 acres, and were tenants on 35 farms totaling 904 acres. In 1942, 106 Japanese owned farms in the county totaling 1,983 acres, while 209 Japanese were tenants on 10,481 acres.[21] According to the 1940 census, however, Japanese farmers were enumerated as follows: 286 tenants, 63 full owners, 23 part owners, and 18

| | Farm Operators | |
Year	White	Nonwhite*
1900	3,965	30
1910	4,353	146
1920	4,814	202
1930	5,975	262
1940	5,193	415
1945	5,821	93
1950	4,900	382

*Nonwhite includes Blacks, Chinese, East Indians, Japanese, and others, but principally Japanese, as indicated in the marked decline of nonwhite operators between 1940 and 1950 and their increase in 1950.

Table 5. Farm Operators in Santa Clara County by Color, 1900–1950.

managers.[22] The census data reveal 86 full and part owners, or twenty-two percent of all Japanese farm operators in the county. That percentage more closely approximates the statewide percentage of twenty-five percent owners in 1940 as shown in Table 5.[23]

Another index of underdevelopment was the instability of tenure and the high rate of mobility. Economist Robert Higgs has shown that the length of stay was a significant factor in the accumulation of capital.[24] In the absence of other data on the stability of farm tenure among the Japanese, we can only project from the experiences of the farmers we interviewed for this book. The best-documented family history for the period spanning the years from 1907 to 1942 is that of Yoshio Ando. The pattern is also representative in that the average number of years on a given farm, 3.9 years, approximates the average from our sample of typical tenant farmers, 3.6 years:

Date	Location	Type of Tenancy
1909-1913	Dry Creek Road	Sharecropping
1913-1916	Meridian Area	Sharecropping
1916-1920	First Street	Cash
1920-1926	Gish Road/Fourth Street	Cash
1926-1928	Los Angeles	Cash
1928-1930	Gish Road	Cash
1931-1937	Oak Hill/Pearl Avenue	Cash
1937	North First Street	Grower

Table 6. Pattern of Tenancy, Ando Family, 1909-1937.[25]

Such mobility during the period of Japanese

dependency is reminiscent of the pattern of migrant labor. The years leading up to World War II, nonetheless, were indeed a time of marked transitions. These resulted from the immigration of Japanese women (who provided the critical labor required for tenancy), the decline in the availability of Japanese workers and the rise in the cost of their labor, and the changes in the valley's political economy. Japanese dependency was achieved through racism, the manipulation of public opinion, and the alien land laws.

The reciprocal of Japanese underdevelopment was white supremacy. Pragmatic gains were registered through the racial rent premium, unconventional tenures, and investments in the land. Yet, despite defining the contours of the struggle, the dominant class could not predict its final outcome. That was determined by the individual and collective resistance of the Japanese farmers.

Clusters and Migrant Tenants, 1907-1920

The first two decades of the twentieth century witnessed the transformation of Japanese farmers in the valley from laborers to tenants and growers. The years were characterized by the emergence of clusters of Japanese farming communities, primarily within the fertile crescent, and by migrant tenancy or the frequent relocation of farms in the quest for self-sufficiency. These two decades comprised the formative period in the development of a distinctive Japanese American community in the Santa Clara Valley. During the early 1920s, despite a resurgence of anti-Japanese activity, Japanese farmers spread to other areas of the valley and became more firmly rooted, diversified their crops and formed marketing cooperatives, and developed farm technologies to suit their special brand of garden farming.

The following map shows the location and relative sizes of Japanese farming clusters in the valley during the 1920s. The map is based primarily on information derived from oral history and, at best, is a rough approximation. Still, it serves as a useful guide for historical reconstruction.

The clusters at Alviso and Agnew were probably the earliest communities of Japanese farmers in the valley. We consider these "genuine" communities because they held a core of families, their residents were settlers rather than migrant workers, and they comprised self-contained social groupings. Most of the daily activity and social intercourse took place within the cluster, and the people considered themselves members of a particular cluster rather than members of a wider group, such as "the Japanese of San Jose," or "the community of Japanese in the Santa Clara Valley." Even Nihonmachi, by 1910 clearly the most dominant center of Japanese commercial and cultural life in the valley, was not the point of reference for farmers in the outlying areas. Farming families usually maintained friendships only with other farming families in that cluster, and visits to Nihonmachi were rare and generally the province of men. Of course, ethnic identification as Japanese was strong and cut across the geographic boundaries, but it would be historically incorrect to assume a single community in the valley during this early period. Further, the community was not monolithic and consisted of diverse and frequently antagonistic interest groups.

These were not the simple products of generational conflicts or "assimilation," but were the results of a more complex interplay of class formation and oppression and resistance.

The Alviso Cluster

The cluster at Alviso centered around Tom Foon Chew's Bayside Cannery. The cannery employed wage workers largely on a seasonal basis, and employed Japanese managers and laborers on its orchards. The layout included the cannery building, bunkhouses for workers, a cold storage plant, the main office, an apple drier, and, to the south, orchards. Additionally, there were Japanese tenant farmers in the cluster (primarily strawberry growers), a Japanese language school, and a store owned by the Funabiki family.

As noted by the Immigration Commission in 1908, at Alviso there were "five colonies with 44 farmers" leasing 273 acres of land.[26] The report added, "Women secure work in the cannery at Alviso, where their earnings, which are on a piece basis, average more than $1 per day."[27] Our earliest oral history account of the Alviso cluster is when the family of Kotaro Omori moved to Alviso in 1913. There, Kotaro and his eldest son, Hisao, worked for a season at Bayside Cannery peeling tomatoes by hand. The cannery labor force, remembered Hisao, consisted of both whites and Asians.[28] According to the Immigration Commission report, the mixed labor force engendered prejudice against the Japanese. "At Alviso. . .strong feeling is exhibited by those who are more or less dependent upon the local cannery against the employment of Asiatics. The cannery

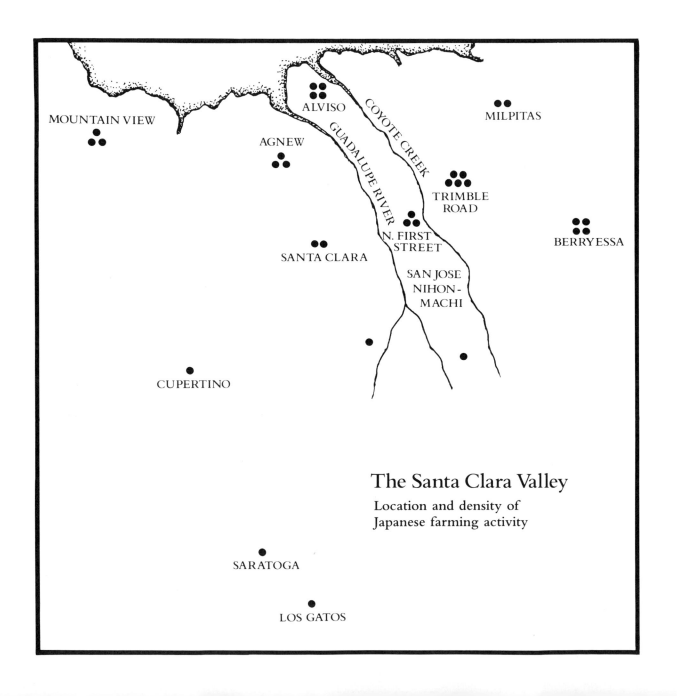

MOUNTAIN VIEW

ALVISO

COYOTE CREEK

MILPITAS

AGNEW

GUADALUPE RIVER

TRIMBLE
ROAD

BERRYESSA

N. FIRST
STREET

SANTA CLARA

SAN JOSE
NIHON-
MACHI

CUPERTINO

The Santa Clara Valley

Location and density of
Japanese farming activity

SARATOGA

LOS GATOS

has for years been controlled by Chinese, and Asiatics predominate among the hands now employed."[29]

Japanese children were apparently denied admission to the public school in nearby Agnew. In 1908, there were between twenty and thirty Japanese children of school age in the area of Agnew and Alviso. Unlike Agnew, these were welcomed at the school in Alviso and were "regarded as very desirable pupils in every way." Japanese farmers contributed to the cost of running the school despite having little or no taxable property. And, besides supporting the public school, Japanese farmers "have also fitted up a school room to serve as a supplementary school, where the Japanese children go each day, at the close of the public-school session, to learn to read and write English [sic] and to acquire the outlines of the history of Japan."[30]

Around 1920, Suyekichi and Misao Takeda leased about five acres from Tom Foon Chew and grew raspberries.[31] After two years, the Takedas bought in the name of George Ikeda, Misao's American-born cousin, ten acres of a young pear orchard adjacent to the Tom Foon property. Sue, the Takeda's eldest daughter, recalled that women labored in all aspects of the farm including household work such as cleaning, cooking, and sewing. Socializing and neighborhood gatherings were rare because of the demanding work schedule. However, just about everyone celebrated New Year's Day in traditional Japanese fashion. It was the largest social event of the year and often lasted for days, or even a week. Homes in the community were open to friends and relatives who visited and feasted from house to house to welcome in the new year.[32]

Around 1927, Tom Foon leased orchard land on the Nelson Ranch on North First Street. Heikichi Ezaki was appointed foreman to manage the property, which grew mainly pear and apple trees. His duties included supervising about forty laborers hired mainly during the harvest season, and keeping an account of the farm. Wages were paid directly from Tom Foon to the workers, although in matters of farming, he relied upon and often consulted with Heikichi. The wage laborers consisted mainly of Filipino and Portuguese men. Bunkhouses were provided for the Filipino migrants on the property, while the Portuguese commuted from their homes in Santa Clara. Tom Foon later hired Masami, Heikichi's eldest son, to manage his leased apricot orchard in the Mount Pleasant area.[33] Other farm enterprises in the Alviso area similarly employed Japanese workers. The Gallagher Fruit Company, for example, maintained about 200 acres of pears and apples during this period with the help of Asian labor. Japanese men were employed in the orchard, while Chinese men, recruited from the Sacramento delta through Chinese labor contractors, did much of the packing in Gallagher's fruit packing house.[34]

Unfortunately, we know very little about the large numbers of Japanese strawberry farms in the Alviso cluster. These were among the most characteristic of the area, and strawberries were one of the major crops grown by Japanese farmers in the cluster. In 1908, for example, of the twenty farms studied by the Immigration Commission in Alviso and Agnew, nineteen grew berries, and sales receipts for that year in berries totaled $6,680 for strawberries and $12,500 for other berries.[35] (Later, during the return period immediately following World War II, strawberries helped in the recovery of many bereft returnees and Japanese contributions to the industry as a whole were considerable.)[36]

Of the nineteen berry farms in 1908, sixteen were held by cash tenants while the remaining three were held by share tenants who received half of the sale.[37] Berries required less land than vegetables for equivalent returns, thus accounting for their attractiveness under cash tenancy. However, strawberries especially required considerable skill to grow and an abundant amount of stoop labor, and although they produced fruit relatively quickly, the plants were productive for only up to four years.[38] Berry production seemed to predominate during this transition period, from around 1900 through 1910, and was centered around the Alviso and Agnew clusters. Because of the advantages, berries seemed well-suited for Japanese farming start-ups and were grown both during the beginning of Japanese tenancy and during the post-World War II recovery period.

The portrait of the Alviso cluster that emerges from the bits and pieces of scattered historical evidence is one of a vibrant Japanese farming community. Japanese farm tenancy first developed in this area of the valley probably because of the allied agricultural industries in the vicinity that employed Japanese farmers as wage laborers to supplement their marginal farm earnings. That feature no doubt facilitated Japanese tenancy, and presumably played a prominent role in the decision of where to settle. Also influential in helping to establish Japanese farmers was their selection of crops — berries. Many of the earliest farmers seem to have gotten their start in this area as berry

growers and then moved on to other places in the valley. At the very least, the Alviso cluster mirrors the composite lives of Japanese farmers in the Santa Clara Valley, first, as a point of arrival on the docks as laborers; then, as a place of settlement for married couples; and finally, as a neighborhood community with a Japanese language school, a store, and group picnics and cultural celebrations.

The Trimble Road Cluster

Radiating from the Alviso and Agnew areas, other Japanese farming clusters appeared. Perhaps among the earliest of these, and certainly one of the largest, was the settlement in the vicinity of Trimble Road. The cluster resembled the Alviso group in a number of ways, and included over thirty families bearing the names of Hashimoto, Hayakawa, Hinaga, Hirose, Honda, Ikegami, Inouye, Kawahara, Kikugawa, Kino, Masunaga, Morimoto, Nakamura, Omori, Ozawa, Sakauye, Santo, and others. At the same time, the Trimble Road cluster had unique characteristics that distinguished it from the Alviso and Agnew clusters. The settlement probably began in 1902 with the NKS Company. The NKS Company was formed by three men from Wakayama *ken* who formed a partnership and grew strawberries on about fifteen acres of rented land. The core of the cluster also included the bachelors and families of the Kino Farm, another Wakayama *ken* venture. The Kino group farmed about twenty-five acres of strawberries and an equal number of acres of garden vegetables until about 1910.

Soon, other families joined the Trimble Road cluster growing strawberries, raspberries, loganberries, and beans. The variety of crops helped to avert total losses for the year in the event of crop failure, and assisted in spreading out the amount of work required over the agricultural year. The plan also resulted in several harvests that in turn meant income at different times of the year. The strategy was well-designed for small-scale operations, especially for farms just starting out, but the crops were labor-intensive and earnings had to be supplemented with wage labor. During the winter months until about April, many of these men and women left their farms to work at the California Packing Corporation (CPC) camp in nearby Milpitas. Here, CPC maintained a boardinghouse for those Japanese laborers who worked on pea farms in the surrounding foothills. CPC hired a Japanese foreman, Henry Yoshihara, who, recalled Katsusaburo Kawahara, rode around in his Stutz car.[39] The Japanese boarders paid CPC for their lodgings, and sometimes, when there were heavy rains, would end up losing money after a season of work.

By the 1920s, the Trimble Road cluster was a vital community. The farmers drew water from Coyote Creek and shared six or seven wells. Nakamura was their *soncho san,* or community leader, who was consulted in disputes and issues affecting the collective group. They maintained a Japanese language school financed in large part by Kiso Yasunaga, wealthy owner of Yasunaga Produce Transfer Company in Nihonmachi, but also supported by the entire community.[40]

The cluster represented another stage in the development of the Japanese farming community in the Santa Clara Valley. Like the Alviso and Agnew clusters, it was sustained by wage labor at the Milpitas CPC camp, and, like the earliest clusters, specialized in berries, mainly strawberries. But beyond that, the Trimble Road cluster had its beginnings in *ken*-based partnerships, perhaps accounting for the informal leadership structure, and the farmers ventured into crop diversification. The movement away from berries and into vegetables and, in a few cases, orchards, is indicative of advancement because those changes required progressively less labor. In turn, they point to the development of permanent communities, greater investments in the land, and more complex relationships.

The West Side, Santa Clara, and Berryessa Clusters

Several fundamental changes took place during the 1920s. Japanese farmers, in their search for better opportunities, relocated to other areas of the valley, forming smaller clusters. These were generally scattered but comprised separate pockets of Japanese farms and communities. For example, Matagoro and Naka Kurasaki first settled in Alviso in 1906. Around 1912, the family moved to the Henrietta Cropley ranch in Berryessa and there farmed garden crops along with other Japanese tenants including the Sasaos. In 1919/1920, the family purchased about eleven acres of prune orchards on the west side, off Saratoga Road. Most of their neighbors in the new location were white ethnics including Italians, Portuguese, and Swedes. The few Japanese families in the area, nonetheless, established a Japanese language school on Payne Avenue during the 1920s, which sometime during the late 1920s or early 1930s, was moved to

Prospect Road. The Japanese language school thus served as a center for the dispersed community in the vicinity.[41]

Families sometimes settled where they were first employed as migrant laborers. Hirokichi Inouye, upon arriving in San Jose around 1900, was employed seasonally on the Hume Ranch in Los Gatos. The ranch consisted of about 400 acres of orchards, primarily prunes but also some apricots. During the winter, Hirokichi went to San Francisco to find work in the city. After several years of this, he became a permanent employee of Hume Ranch and in 1910 was promoted to foreman of the Japanese work crew. All of the farm laborers were Japanese with one exception, a white man who took care of the farm equipment. The workers lived in bunkhouses on the ranch. During the peak season, the ranch employed as many as seventy workers, while during the winter, only a skeleton crew of ten to fifteen was maintained.

In 1919, in anticipation of the impending division and sale of the Hume Ranch, Hirokichi formed the Glenhill Farming Corporation. In order to evade the alien land law, he made his American-born sons, Kaoru, Tatsuru, and Tohru, the trustees. The corporation was thus able to purchase over fourteen acres of the available property. The Inouye family was one of only a few Japanese families living in the Los Gatos area. The others included the Nishimura and Oka families. Because of their small numbers, those Japanese belonged to the west side cluster, sending their children to the Payne Avenue Japanese language school.[42]

Other Japanese farming clusters appeared in the Santa Clara and Berryessa townships. There were about a dozen Japanese farms in the Santa Clara area during the 1920s and 1930s, including those of the Higuchi, Matsumoto, Nakamura, Nakano, Ono, Sakamoto, and Sawabe families. A Japanese language school was established at Scott and Kifer, and Asanuma, an insurance agent, served as teacher. Japanese peddlers came from San Jose Nihonmachi to sell groceries and Japanese foodstuffs to the Santa Clara farmers. Because of the small number of Japanese in the area, most looked to Nihonmachi for recreation and entertainment. Still, the circle of friends for social interaction centered around the immediate cluster.[43]

The Berryessa cluster, including the twenty families on the McGinty and Brandt ranches, grew a diversity of garden crops and shared in the cost of drilling and maintaining wells. Kechizo and Kane Matsumura, residing on JUF (Jim Uyeda Farm) No. 1, farmed beans, bell peppers, broccoli, cucumbers, lettuce, raspberries, spinach, squash, and tomatoes. Such diversity enabled virtually year-round cultivation and income for the family. The farmers of the cluster shared horses, implements, and, on occasion, their hired laborers. The Matsumuras, along with three other farmers, shared a common well. A schedule was drawn up for its daily use, a log was kept of the hours used by each farmer, and when the monthly bill arrived, the group gathered at a member's home to settle the account and socialize. A Japanese language school was built on Yamaichi's property, and, as in Santa Clara, peddlers from Nihonmachi came by to sell tofu, fresh fish, and other foodstuffs.[44]

Evolution of Marketing Strategies

The 1920s thus witnessed the emergence and

growth of new Japanese farming clusters spreading from the original clusters at Alviso and Agnew. These satellite communities bore the characteristics of their progenitors but also evolved distinctive traits of their own. Other changes in Japanese farming in the valley during the 1920s reflected the growing complexity of farm operations, primarily in the area of marketing.

As Japanese farmers moved from share tenancy to cash tenancy and ownership, the advantages of marketing cooperatives became clear. At first, individual farmers made their own arrangements for the sale of their crops. These sales involved both Japanese and non-Japanese middlemen. Independent truckers in San Jose, including Yasunaga, de Marco, and the Hinaga brothers, collected packed produce from the various Japanese farms and took them to commission houses in San Francisco and Oakland. The commission houses paid the truckers, charged a commission of ten percent plus expenses on the sale, and sent the remainder back to the farmers. Sometimes the produce would be dumped if the shipment was not sold that day, and the farmer would receive nothing.[45]

Eventually, as the area's Japanese farm produce became known, buyers from San Francisco, Oakland, Sacramento, and even Los Angeles came to the Santa Clara Valley. These buyers paid the farmers in cash, especially if the quality of the produce and the demand for it was high. At other times, they would place orders with the farmers and pay on consignment. The Berryessa cluster was, on occasion, visited by trucker Paul Dildine, an employee of a Chinese-owned commission house in Sacramento called General Produce. This buyer had a reputation for paying good prices and in cash.[46] The Los Angeles wholesalers, both Japanese and white, even maintained a dock on Trimble Road where farmers from the surrounding clusters could bring their produce for sale. Vegetables and fruits grown in the valley were profitable in Los Angeles because of the seasonal variations between northern and southern California. Despite the higher shipping costs, the Los Angeles buyers offered better prices than those in the Bay Area because the demand was greater in Los Angeles. Furthermore, the Japanese wholesalers there charged lower fees than the Italian-controlled commission houses in the Bay Area.[47]

Cooperatives and Class Formation, 1920s and 1930s

Agricultural cooperatives were formed early in the history of Japanese farmers in the valley and were another indication of increasing complexity in the evolution of the farming community. Perhaps the earliest was the Japanese Agricultural Alliance in Agnew, which was established before 1908. The Immigration Commission report described the cooperative: "The Japanese Agricultural Alliance is a purely local organization of farmers about Agnews. Its object is to promote the interests of these farmers and, in such ways as are open to it, to care for those who are in distress. Practically all of the tenant farmers of the locality are members of this alliance."[48] The Alliance, thus, was not simply an economic association but also served a social and cultural function.

Japanese ethnic cooperation in America originated in Japan from collectivity, a cardinal cultural value, and from like organizations common to farming communities.[49] However, Japanese collective behavior in America underwent significant modification. Japanese agricultural cooperatives in the Santa Clara Valley, for example, eventually came to focus almost exclusively on the economic self-interest of their members, reflecting the wider setting of American capitalism. Further, their rise and eventual demise offer clues of class formation within the Japanese farming community and of the dependent community's position in the valley's political economy.

The San Jose Bushberry Association was founded in 1916 and lasted until 1922 when it splintered into two groups, one at Wayne Station on Oakland Road, the other in Nihonmachi. The originators of the Association were not farmers themselves but Nihonmachi businessmen like Okagaki. The members, Japanese berry farmers, paid a percentage of their sales to the Association; this in turn was used to support a salaried secretary. The principal benefit for the member was group marketing; the Association did not engage in extending credit or bulk buying.[50] Gunki Kai described the Association:

> The Japanese berry-growers in the vicinity of San Jose have an association whose membership totaling 32 [sic]. They own a market in the Japanese section of San Jose, to which all the berries are sent and merchants from San Francisco and Oakland come to buy them. The market is opened every evening, except Saturday. The total transaction during a week amounts to from $5,000 to $10,000. Due to its small size, everything is managed by one paid secretary, whose salary is $125 a month.

He studies market conditions, keeps accounts, and does all the other incidental works. Out of each transaction 6 per cent is subtracted to provide for the office and upkeep expenses, and the salary of the secretary.[51]

Japanese farmers at Alviso, including Nitahara, Oshio, Sakamoto, and Uyemura, formed a celery cooperative with a shed and a buyers' cooperative called Kobai Kumiai. During the Great Depression years, the cooperative facilitated bulk purchases of fertilizers and sprays.[52] During the 1930s, a Trimble Road cooperative was established mainly for marketing and purchasing. About thirty-two families in the cluster were members of the cooperative, which operated up to World War II with a voluntary secretary.[53]

Clearly, however, the most ambitious Japanese agricultural cooperative in the valley was the Celery Growers' Association begun in 1931 by Tomiju Takeda, a remarkable Issei pioneer who quite possibly originated celery growing among Japanese farmers. Takeda arrived in the United States in 1907. He worked as a dishwasher in logging camps in the state of Washington, and as a kitchen helper at a hotel in Bellingham. His son, Shoji, described his first encounter with celery while working at the hotel:

> On this assignment as a salad cook, there was one vegetable that he was not allowed to handle, which was celery. This caused his curiosity to be aroused. He...asked the chief of the waiters, as to why the vegetable celery was so sacred. The answer was that celery is a very rare commodity, difficult to grow on the

Pacific Coast..., and a very minute number of growers produce this crop. Therefore, celery is expensive, extraordinary in terms of commodity, rare and many people did not know how to eat this product.[54]

The experience piqued his interest in celery and he determined to specialize in the crop. Takeda moved to the Santa Clara Valley in around 1909, working as a migrant laborer and in the off-season as a caretaker at Stanford University. While at Stanford he chanced upon a field of celery belonging to a Chinese farmer. "This celery field, though small in size, interested my father very much as to the type of operation. Therefore, he religiously visited this Chinese grower who welcomed him and explained to the best of his knowledge about the production of celery."[55] Neither could speak the other's language but through hand signs and written notes in Chinese and Japanese they were able to communicate.[56]

That unnamed Chinese farmer, skilled in the cultivation of celery, was instrumental in introducing an important new crop to the valley's Japanese farmers. In 1914, Tomiju Takeda rented ten acres in the Alviso area and planted celery. The first few years were difficult:

One problem was that although the area was ideally suited for the production of celery, flooding occurred because of being in the low lands near the south bay. In the winter of the first year during the harvest season, heavy rains came and flooded the crop half way through harvest. After the flood, motivation still persisted my father to harvest the remainder of the crop by digging out the remaining celery by shovel, one by one, transporting them to the edge of the field, where he washed each head of celery in a stream of artesian water that was flowing. Then he packed the celery into crates and delivered them to the Port of Alviso. From there the celery was transported to San Francisco by boat. Although being very painful and difficult work, he had to do this to survive.[57]

Before long, other Japanese farmers took up the crop. Celery grown in the Santa Clara Valley was soon preferred over that produced in the Stockton area. The latter had predominated in the San Francisco markets but had an unpleasant odor because it was grown in "muck soil."[58] The Santa Clara Valley celery, on the other hand, had no offensive odor, was sweet and crisp, and consequently commanded higher prices. That opportunity for profits in turn encouraged more Japanese farmers to grow celery, resulting in an overproduction of the crop and depressed prices. Shoji Takeda described the situation:

Since Santa Clara Valley celery became known for its high quality and top of the market prices received, many neighboring growers started to inquire about celery production from Tomiju Takeda.... Therefore, my father gave information to these growers which caused the celery production in this valley to greatly expand in acreage. This, in turn, created new problems in marketing celery to the area markets. The problems were such as the growers were sending products to numerous wholesale terminal houses with vast differences in individual packaging causing their own competition. Sometime after, my father called the growers together for a general growers meeting to discuss matters and to analyze the problems with them and to put into effect counter measures to relieve this condition.[59]

The meeting involved prominent celery growers like Yoshio Ando, Katsusaburo Kawahara, and Yukichi Oyama, and, from the Trimble Road and Alviso clusters, Kawashima, Okutani, and Suyekichi Takeda. The group discussed the advantages of forming a celery marketing cooperative and strategies for maximizing profits. They concluded that they would select and deal with only the two or three San Francisco commission houses that offered the best prices, they would regulate their output to avoid flooding the market, and they would work to secure another outlet beyond the Bay Area to sell their excess or overage.[60] Additionally, Tomiju Takeda urged uniform packaging and quality controls so Santa Clara Valley celery would continue to fetch high prices.[61] Thus the Celery Growers' Association, an informal alliance of Japanese farmers in the valley, was formed in 1931.

Yoshio Ando was asked to be the first director of the Association on a voluntary basis, and after two years, the group hired a secretary. The Association had about twenty-seven members who paid a penny on every crate of celery handled by the cooperative, while buyers paid an additional penny per crate.[62] The Association marked a significant departure from the first Japanese agricultural

cooperatives because its members came from several clusters thus cutting across regional boundaries, and because it developed markets outside the Bay Area in cities like Chicago and New York. These sales were handled by brokerage houses in San Jose that shipped the celery to the East Coast on consignment. Because the brokers required a steady supply, Association members had to set aside a certain portion of their production for that market. Sometimes the profits were greater through the brokerage handlers; at other times, the Bay Area markets yielded better returns. The problems associated with shipping celery to the East Coast included the twenty percent commission charged by most brokers, and the delay in receiving payment on goods sent on consignment, usually seven to ten days.[63]

Despite those drawbacks, the larger celery growers — Ando, Kawahara, and Takeda — profited from the arrangement because of their considerable overage. The smaller farmers, mostly tenants, could not afford the delayed cash flow and saw little benefits for them in the marketing scheme. After about three or four years, the three principals were voted out of the Association by the small growers, and the Association languished and eventually died.

Still, the Celery Growers' Association was an extraordinary development in the history of Japanese farmers in the valley. It drew members from different clusters, it extended the market for Japanese-produced crops to the East Coast,[64] and it sought, through a two-tiered marketing scheme, to increase production without the consequent lowering of prices through glutting. The formation of the Association revealed the singular object of its members: profits. The profits in turn provided the glue which bound them together. Conversely, the split several years later showed the most prominent dividing line within its ranks, capital. The conflict between the owners of capital and those essentially devoid of capital resulted in the noteworthy, albeit unsuccessful, revolt of the smaller farmers. The Association, thus, was not an example of ethnic solidarity per se, but instead mirrored the wider realities of American capitalism. It also points to incipient class formation within the ethnic farming community and to conflict and competition based on self-interest, not collectivity, among the Japanese in America.

Another source of conflict in the Celery Growers' Association involved greenhouses, which only the larger growers could afford. Yoshio Ando introduced greenhouses to the Japanese farmers in the valley. While in Los Angeles, Ando noticed their widespread use by Japanese farmers but did not fully appreciate their importance. He returned to the Santa Clara Valley in 1928 and ordered celery seedlings from Suetake Nursery in Culver City in west Los Angeles. The nursery sent his order but suggested that he grow his own seedlings in San Jose to save on the expense of shipping them from Los Angeles. The following year, Ando built an experimental greenhouse and over the years refined its construction for his specific needs. Redwood lumber and glass were the materials used to build greenhouses 28 feet by 100 feet in dimension, with raised platforms 2 feet off the ground for the seedling trays. Even the width and length of the platforms were carefully measured to fit the dimensions of the trays so there would be no wasted space. He also placed a steam boiler in

the greenhouse to provide heat during the winter, and installed faucets for running water for the seedlings.[65]

Tomiju Takeda and Katsusaburo Kawahara followed Yoshio Ando's lead and built three or four greenhouses each for their celery seedlings. The advantages provided by greenhouses in celery growing was more than simple savings on seedling purchases from commercial nurseries. Normally, celery seeds were directly planted in the field after the threat of frost had passed. These were permitted to grow for three to four months before they were transplanted to another field. With greenhouses, seedlings developed in thirty days, and these were then transplanted into larger trays and permitted to grow for another month in the greenhouse. By the first of March, they would be vigorous and ready for transplanting in the fields. Thus, greenhouses permitted earlier plantings of celery, shortened the growing time, and minimized the tendency of the plant to bolt.[66] The larger growers were able to capitalize on those benefits and prospered even more. The smaller farmers, on the other hand, saw greenhouses as a privilege of the wealthier growers, and some began rumors in an attempt to strike back at what they perceived as unfair competition. The rumors included the notion that tomato and bellpepper seedlings grown in greenhouses did not produce fruit; farmers, accordingly, should not buy those seedlings from the three growers.

Contrary to the idea of ethnic solidarity, that sort of behavior was apparently more typical than exceptional. Yoshio Ando, while living in Los Angeles in 1926, was sold ten to twelve acres of blighted celery, unknown to him but known to the previous Japanese owner. Ando lost considerable money in the deal as the entire crop had to be dumped. The following season, his neighbors refused to sell him seedlings in January and February, the best months for planting, but he was finally able to obtain seedlings in March. When he harvested his crop in July, no local buyers would touch it so Ando ended up shipping his produce to the Bay Area.[67] In the Santa Clara Valley, there were instances in which Japanese farmers deliberately sabotaged the fields of other farmers by destroying the plants. Others worked to develop special cultivating techniques, which, if proven successful, were not shared with their neighbors. The farmers attributed such behavior to a keen sense of competition among Japanese farmers in general rather than to individual feuds and jealousies. If true, they offer examples of typical capitalistic economic behavior.

Dependency Reaffirmed

By the 1920s, Japanese farmers were firmly established in the Santa Clara Valley. The State Board of Control reported that Japanese farmers produced sixty percent of the tomatoes delivered to canneries in the valley, eighty-two percent of the spinach, and one hundred percent of "other vegetables."[68] Sawyer recorded in 1922 that "strawberry cultivation has been undertaken north of Berryessa. In late years, large tracts have been leased by the Japanese and Chinese, who now control the bulk of production."[69] The 1920s and 1930s saw the spread of Japanese farming communities or clusters throughout the valley, especially along the fertile crescent. The period also

witnessed the rise of Japanese agricultural cooperatives designed to reduce their members' costs and increase their profits.

Despite that apparent progress, the position of Japanese farmers vis-a-vis the valley's political economy was made eminently clear when the Japanese-owned Santa Clara Produce Canning Company and the California Commercial Corporation filed for incorporation in October of 1920. The Japanese exclusion committee of the San Jose post of the American Legion got wind of the proposal and orchestrated a campaign to prevent the incorporation from taking place. The committee threatened to bring the matter to California Attorney General U.S. Webb, and urged local unions not to aid in the construction of the Japanese canneries. The drive was successful and the canneries were not built.[70]

The construction of the canneries would have been a major breakthrough for the Japanese American communities in the valley. They would have provided employment for local Japanese residents, and probably would have attracted a good number of other Japanese to the area. They also would have meant a measure of Japanese control over the commercial marketing of their farm commodities and a way of by-passing the monopoly held by a few dominant canneries in the valley, including the California Packing Corporation. But beyond that, the canneries could have forged a formidable economic complex involving Japanese farms, transportation systems, and perhaps expansion into other areas. We had a local example in the Bayside Cannery of Tom Foon Chew, which sustained a comparatively large Japanese community in the Alviso and Agnew areas. Another good example was the Japanese farm and produce network in the Los Angeles basin. Clearly, that scenario could not be tolerated in the Santa Clara Valley during this historical period. The Japanese presence, while permanent, was designed to profit the dominant class; Japanese dependency was sought and maintained.

Self-Determination Asserted

While the prevailing social relations were predicated upon Japanese dependency, as in the period of migrant labor, there were numerous assertions of self-determination. These included the immigration of Japanese women and the addition of their labor to the household unit of production, strategies for higher wages and the rise in the cost of Japanese labor, the formation of Japanese farm corporations and Nisei-headed "camps," the emergence of farm clusters and development of permanent communities, and farm partnerships and marketing cooperatives.

A survey of divorce cases in the county between 1900 and 1942 uncovered twenty involving Japanese. Of these, fourteen were initiated by women.[71] It is impossible, of course, to generalize on the precise meaning of those statistics. It is surprising, nonetheless, to have found so many divorces among Japanese in the county during that period. Especially revealing is the number of Japanese women pursuing legal separation from their husbands. This finding merits further study because it contradicts conventional cultural interpretations of the pre-war Japanese American communities, and because it exemplifies pervasive social forces and changes such as the growing and

substantial economic importance of women in the family.

Farming innovations and inventions constituted another kind of assertion on the part of Japanese farmers. These were largely the products of their own ingenuity employed in the struggle to overcome disadvantages inherent in their situation of dependency. For example, Japanese farmers were regularly offered marginal lands such as swampy and hilly areas. Their problem was compounded with their selection of crops — garden vegetables — which required frequent and even watering. The choice was not fortuitous but was dictated by the needs of the dominant society. Japanese farmers were tolerated insofar as they posed no economic threat to the valley's orchards, and were desired during this period of dependency because they provided several opportunities for pragmatic gains. For the Japanese farmers, however, the sloping land — tilted in favor of the dominant class — had to be leveled if their gardens were to prosper.

The development of the Japanese leveler revealed the skillfulness of Japanese farmers but also symbolized their drive for self-determination. It evolved from the "Fresno scraper," probably originating in Fresno and consisting of an iron scoop drawn by horses. The Fresno scraper simply removed high spots on the field. The excess dirt collected in the scoop was dumped at the end of the row, and each row was comparatively short, about fifty or sixty feet in length, because of the inefficiency of the tool. The Japanese leveler was an improvement in that it permitted leveling of both high and low spots on the field. The leveler consisted of an iron blade mounted on a wood frame structure which held a handle for directing the instrument and a chain hitch for horses. With the Japanese leveler, rows were lengthened to about a hundred feet, but the leveler deposited excess soil along both sides of the blade, requiring several sweeps of the field. A final version, appearing during the 1930s, was the "box leveler," which was a true leveler. It was apparently a local invention and had several variations. The main elements in the box leveler included an iron blade that could be raised and lowered using a lever, a box set on steel runners that stored excess dirt scraped from high spots and later deposited it in depressions, and a platform on the box to enable the operator to ride instead of walking behind the tool. The box leveler permitted rows well over a hundred feet in length. It was indispensible in the cultivation of garden crops, especially celery, and helped to maximize yields.[72]

Scrapers and levelers were primarily identified with Japanese farming because they were designed for small, labor-intensive farms. Commercial tractors and rigs were much too expensive for most Japanese farmers and were manufactured for larger acreages and different types of crops. Japanese farmers adapted the existing technologies to meet their unique needs. Their plans were taken to white blacksmiths such as the Windsor Brothers in Milpitas who in turn produced the Japanese leveler and box leveler for sale to the local farmers. Shoji Takeda drew up plans for a row sprayer based on a modified potato sprayer and took these to a John Bean representative in 1923. Existing sprayers were unsuitable for Japanese farms because they were unwieldy for row crops and lacked the necessary clearance for taller vegetables such as celery. The Bean Company subsequently produced that sprayer and sold it successfully on the West Coast.[73]

Self-Determination Denied

The transition to mechanization would have been the next phase in the development of Japanese farms in the valley. But World War II interrupted that progression when the Japanese farmers were forcibly removed from the valley and placed in America's concentration camps. The years of confinement were not simply lost in terms of marking time. Japanese farmers regressed, absolutely and in most cases unalterably, because the wartime boom enabled mechanization and the nature of the market was transformed. When the Japanese farmers returned to the valley after the war they were faced with a dramatically different and unfamiliar agricultural landscape. They were like Urashima Taro of Japanese legend (the equivalent of Rip Van Winkle) returning to his home after a long absence. They no longer recognized the valley, and the valley's residents largely failed to recognize or acknowledge their existence.

Field workers, men and women, on the Morita farm in Gilroy. Women worked in nearly all phases of farm labor and were especially skilled in certain aspects including berry-picking, fruit-sorting, and thinning out the young plants.
Courtesy of Helen Morishita.

Filipino workers during celery harvest time on the Takeda farm in 1930. Japanese farmers, beginning in the 1920s, increasingly turned to non-Japanese farm laborers, principally Filipinos and Mexicans.
Courtesy of Hiroshi Takeda.

Planting tomatoes on Alviso Road, c.1928. Women, using short-handle hoes, did the backbreaking labor of transplanting. Also notice the young boy holding the seedlings.
Courtesy of Misaye Santo.

Packing spinach on Alviso Road, 1928. Notice the large crates with the California Packing Corporation stamp, and the involvement of men and women in the work.
Courtesy of Misaye Santo.

Yuwakichi Sakauye's 20 acre farm on Trimble Road, c.1910. Sakauye purchased the farm with profits made from strawberry sharecropping in 1907, and planted pears, apricots, and prunes and intercropped beans, peppers, spinach, strawberries, and *daikon* (Japanese radish) between the rows of young fruit trees. In the foreground are Yuwakichi, Tamae, and their four children, Eiichi, Kenji, Ayako, and Kimi.
Courtesy of Eiichi Sakauye.

Tenant farmer, Riichi Nishimura, rented this farm on Spring Street in San Jose. The photograph was taken in 1913.
Courtesy of Hideko Morishita.

The Takeda farm purchased in 1932 on the Barber Ranch. Notice the farmhouses, the water tank, the large greenhouses, and reservoir in the foreground. Pictured from left to right are Chizu Takeda and son, Hiroshi, Shoji Takeda on the tractor, and George, Issei pioneer Tomiju Takeda, and Shin on the platform. *Courtesy of Hiroshi Takeda.*

Chizu Takeda and sons, Hiroshi (in her arms) and Shin (in car).
The photograph was taken in 1931 on the Abel Ranch. Notice the
greenhouse behind the wash hanging out to dry.
Courtesy of Hiroshi Takeda.

The Kawahara family built this
home on Brokaw Road, San Jose,
in 1936, on land leased from the
county tax collector, O'Brien.
Mrs. Kawahara is seen far left and
Mr. Kawahara far right.
*Courtesy of Kawahara Family, California
History Center Archives.*

Ploughing between the fruit trees on the Ando farm on North First Street. This picture was probably taken in the late 1930s.
Courtesy of Yoshio Ando.

Spreading chicken manure on the Takeda farm. Tomiju Takeda was one of the first Issei farmers to use organic fertilizers. Yoshio Ando sent his truck up to Hayward to collect manure from the poultry farms there. Other farmers used fish meal from Japan. These organic substitutes were cheaper than commercial fertilizers and enabled the Issei farmers to keep the costs down. This picture was taken in 1938. Dick Matsui is driving the tractor and Mr. Moraga is spreading the manure.
Courtesy of Hiroshi Takeda.

Kuniaki Hidaka cultivating spinach on his farm in Coyote in 1925. Horses had to be specially trained to follow the rows without damaging the crops. Notice the unidentified man field-packing the spinach into crates.
Courtesy of William Hidaka.

Topping sugar beets in the Coyote area. The tractor was used to unearth the sugar beets, the workers followed behind and removed the tops with knives, and the beets were placed in the horse-drawn cart.
Courtesy of William M. Hidaka.

Drying pears on the Sakauye farm in 1933. The Sakauyes belonged the the Santa Clara Pear Growers Association and a fruit marketing coop which consisted mainly of white farmers and a few Japanese Americans.
Courtesy of Eiichi Sakauye.

Riichi Nishimura at the corner of Sixth and Jackson Streets in San Jose Nihonmachi in 1910. Nishimura is delivering his produce to market.
Courtesy of Hideko Morishita.

Wayne Basket Company, begun in 1910 by Kamejiro Shimizu, was the first berry basket-making company in the Santa Clara Valley. The original structure was located at Wayne Station on the Old Oakland Highway. This picture was taken around 1920 and shows the machine in the background which produced sheets of wood shavings and the machine in the foreground which transformed those shavings into baskets.
Courtesy of Grant Shimizu.

Yukino Ezaki (l) and friend (r) sorting pears in 1920. Women worked in the orchard alongside their husbands in addition to their domestic labor. Notice the Bayside Cannery Company boxes.
Courtesy of Tom Ezaki.

Mr. Ishizaki taking tomatoes to the cannery, 1918. Japanese farmers relied primarily on independent truckers to take their produce to market.
Courtesy of Harry Nishiura.

San Jose Produce Market at Market and San Fernando Streets around 1905. Shigekichi Kawashima was one of the first Issei farmers to sell his produce at the open market. Farmers arrived as early as 4 a.m. and sold their produce by 7 a.m. The San Jose market offered an alternative to the San Francisco and Oakland produce houses.
Courtesy of Eiichi Sakauye.

Monterey Fish Market or Shiromoto Sakanaya on Sixth Street in San Jose Nihonmachi.
Courtesy of Ayako Kamachi.

Alviso Japanese language school on New Year's Day, c.1930. Group picture of language school pupils and their parents. Japanese language schools in the outlying farming clusters were largely built and supported by the local Japanese community.
Courtesy of Sueko Hirai.

Laundry owned by Hatakeyama in Saratoga. Japanese-owned businesses gradually spread beyond Nihon-machi to other areas of the valley. These then became the foci of the outlying Japanese clusters.
Courtesy of Ayako Kamachi.

Kinokuniya Shoten or grocery store owned by Kinosuke Dobashi located on Jackson Street in San Jose Nihonmachi. The store sold mainly Japanese foodstuffs including fresh and salted fish and vegetables. This photograph was taken around 1910. Contrast this with the picture in Chapter 6 of the Old Santo Market taken around 1946.

Courtesy of California History Center Archives.

Okita Brothers Store located on Fifth and Jackson Streets in San Jose Nihonmachi. This store and its branch in Campbell served the outlying Japanese farm clusters. The photograph was taken around 1920. Notice the distinctly Japanese goods sold by the store.
Courtesy of California History Center Archives.

Original Buddhist Church on Sixth Street in San Jose's Nihonmachi. The church was officially recognized in August 1902.
Courtesy of Nishiura Family, Kanemoto Collection, California History Center Archives.

Farm family probably on their way to San Jose Nihonmachi. Such visits, especially as a family outing, were rare since most of the social activity revolved around the farm cluster.
Courtesy of Grant Shimizu.

Funeral at the original Buddhist temple on Sixth Street in San Jose Nihonmachi. Funerals were one of the primary functions of the Buddhist church in America, reinforcing Japanese values of collectivity (family and community) and ancestor worship. This picture was taken in 1922.
Courtesy of California History Center Archives.

Group destined for Japan in front of Taihei-yokan in San Jose's Nihonmachi, 1927.
Courtesy of H. Taketa Family, California History Center Archives.

Shimane *ken* picnic in the orchard in spring. Note the development of families and children, the Nisei. This photograph was taken in c.1920.
Courtesy of Misaye Santo.

Kenjinkai (prefectural) picnic, c.1920. The 1920s was a transition period from "bachelor society" to permanent communities. Note the mixture of young men (comprising the majority of the group), women, and couples with infants.

Courtesy of Nishimura Family, California History Center Archives.

Japanese language school children's play at Okita Hall in San Jose Nihonmachi. The picture was taken around 1925. Japanese language schools were not only transmitters of language skills; they also promoted Japanese culture.
Courtesy of Kifune Family, California History Center Archives.

Mas Kifune in baseball uniform. The photograph was taken looking north on Sixth Street in San Jose Nihon-machi around 1921. Notice the storefronts, unpaved dirt road, and the drainage ditch.
Courtesy of Ayako Kamachi.

The San Jose Asahi Baseball Team, 1922. The team was made up from all star players from San Francisco, Salinas, Fresno and other towns. They were well known, eventually invited to Japan with manager Okagaki.
Courtesy of Kawahara Family, Kanemoto Collection, California History Center Archives.

Cultural instruction was important to the Japanese community. Shown here is the *koto* class, San Jose in the 1930s with Mrs. Medori Kifune at far left.
Courtesy of Kifune Family, California History Center Archives.

Sumo tournament in San Jose Nihonmachi. A sumo ring was constructed on the open field at Sixth and Jackson. Large crowds were attracted to these tournaments frequently featuring visiting wrestlers.
Courtesy of Bill Kogura.

Young Men's Buddhist Association Band.
Courtesy of Kifune Family, California History Center Archives.

Oku Nursery, Mountain View. Unosuke Oku arrived in America from Wakayama, Japan in 1886. In 1902, he purchased 6 acres in Mountain View near Baily and Wright Avenues, where it still stands today. During World War II the Oku family chose to move inland to Denver, Colorado, rather being confined in a concentration camp. After the war, the Oku's returned to their farm. As the years progressed, the family diversified types of flowers grown, and expanded their holdings into Half Moon Bay.
Courtesy of Oku Family, California History Center Archives.

Yonemoto Nursery (1930–1935), view from California Avenue, facing northeast with the Mount Hamilton Range in the far distance. Japanese families continued through the twentieth century as major flower growers in the Santa Clara Valley. One such family was the Yonemotos. Tsunegusa Yonemoto arrived from Japan in 1905. He originally leased two acres of land from Murphy near Murphy Avenue in Sunnyvale, built a greenhouse and grew chrysanthemums. In 1915, Tsunegusa was able to buy 18 acres between Mathilda, Arquez, Murphy and California Avenues in the name of his native born son Fred.
Courtesy of Fred Yonemoto, California History Center Archives.

Interior of greenhouse, Oku Nursery, Mountain View. To combat soil disease which develops after each planting, the old soil was removed by hand from the trays and replaced. This expensive, laborious process was later replaced by heat (steam) sterilization of the soil.
Courtesy of Oku Family, California History Center Archives.

Spraying carnations, Yonemoto Nursery.
Courtesy of Fred Yonemoto, California History Center Archives.

Interior glass house with carnations, Yonemoto family, 1940.
Courtesy of Fred Yonemoto, California History Center Archives.

Jiichiro Yonemoto and daughter Kiiko in sorting and bunching shed, 1940.
Courtesy of Fred Yonemoto, California History Center Archives.

Yonemoto family fishing outing on San Francisco Bay, c.1930s. According to Fred, "when striped bass were a plenty and the limit per day was 5 fish."
Courtesy of Fred Yonemoto, California History Center Archives.

Yonemoto Nursery, Sunnyvale, 1940. Relaxing moments in the backyard in front of bamboo trees. Left to right: Gooch, Tsune, Noboru, Kiiko, Tsunegusa, Fred T., Jiichiro, Sumio, Tak.
Courtesy of Fred Yonemoto, California History Center Archives.

Footnotes

[1] Oral History, John Hayakawa, February 24, 1984, and March 2, 1984.

[2] Oral History, Satoru Kawashima, January 12, 1984.

[3] Y. Ichihashi, "Supplementary Report on the Japanese in the Watsonville District," Yamato Ichihashi Papers, Stanford University Archives, SC 71, Box 2, Folder 2.

[4] Oral History, John Hayakawa, February 24, 1984, and March 2, 1984.

[5] Immigration Commission, *Reports,* XXIV, 41-42; and H.A. Millis, *The Japanese Problem in the United States,* Macmillan Company: New York, 1915, 118-19.

[6] Misawa (ed.), *Beginnings,* 26. See also, Oral History, Satoru Kawashima, January 19, 1984.

[7] *San Jose Mercury,* January 8, 1920.

[8] *San Jose Mercury,* August 29, 1919. J.J. McDonald, president of the Santa Clara County Farm Owners' and Operators' Association, similarly favored bringing in bonded Chinese labor, according to the *Daily Palo Alto Times,* January 29, 1920.

[9] Jean Pajus, *The Real Japanese California,* James H. Gillick: Berkeley, 1937, 130-34.

[10] Quoted in Audrie Girdner and Anne Loftis, *The Great Betrayal: The Evacuation of the Japanese-Americans During World War II,* Macmillan Company: London, 1969, 64-65.

[11] *Japanese Immigration,* Hearings, Committee on Immigration and Naturalization, U.S. House of Representatives, 66th Congress, 2d Session, Government Printing Office: Washington, D.C., 1921, 420-24.

[12] Oral History, Eiichi Sakauye, April 27, 1983.

[13] Oral History, Eiichi Sakauye, May 4, 1983.

[14] Oral History, Phil Y. Matsumura, February 16, 1984.

[15] Oral History, Katsusaburo Kawahara, January 25, 1984.

[16] Oral History, Hisao Omori, November 15, 1983.

[17] Shoji Takeda, "Autobiography and Biography," unpubl. manuscript, 9-10.

[18] For a more positive portrayal of O'Brien, see Girdner and Loftis, *Great Betrayal,* 62.

[19] Oral History, Shoji Takeda, December 29, 1983.

[20] Oral History, Shoji Takeda, December 29, 1983.

[21] We are indebted to Sucheng Chan for sharing with us the study from which those totals derive: "Santa Clara County, Ownership Statistics as of March 1, 1942," Records of Adon Poli, No. 285, Preliminary Inventory of the Records of the Bureau of Agricultural Economics, Record Group 83, National Archives. See also, Sharon E. Ray, "Santa Clara County and the Alien Land Initiative of 1920," a paper presented to the California Pioneers Society of Santa Clara County, June 1, 1963, 13; and *Japanese Immigration,* Hearings, House, 66th Congress, 2d Session, 87.

[22] *San Jose Mercury Herald,* March 9, 1942.

[23] Edward K. Strong, Jr., *Japanese in California,* Stanford University Press: Stanford, 1933, 138; Robert Higgs, "Landless by Law: Japanese Immigrants in California Agriculture to 1941," *Journal of Economic History,* 38:1 (March 1978), 222; and Leonard Bloom and Ruth Riemer, *Removal and Return: The Socio-Economic Effects of the War on Japanese Americans,* University of California Press: Berkeley, 1949, 69-70.

[24] Robert Higgs, "The Wealth of Japanese Tenant Farmers in California, 1909," *Agricultural History,* 53:1 (January 1979), 488-93.

[25] Oral History, Yoshio Ando, October 26, 1983, and November 2 and 11, 1983.

[26] Immigration Commission, *Reports,* XXIV, 445.

[27] Immigration Commission, *Reports,* XXIV, 448.

[28] Oral History, Hisao Omori, November 2, 1983.

[29] Immigration Commission, *Reports,* XXIV, 451.

[30] Immigration Commission, *Reports,* XXIV, 451.

[31] Berries had been pioneered in the vicinity during the nineteenth century by the Chinese, although they had long since vanished. Katsusaburo Kawahara recalled a large blackberry farm along Taylor and Hedding owned by Ku Lee around 1911, and the farm of Wo Lee on Gish Road. The farms employed several Chinese men, who wore bamboo guards on their arms to protect them from the thorns. Oral History, Katsusaburo Kawahara,

January 25, 1984.

[32] Oral History, Sue Matsumura, February 23, 1984.

[33] Oral History, Tom Ezaki, January 27, 1984, and February 2, 1984.

[34] Oral History, John Hayakawa, February 24, 1984, and March 2, 1984.

[35] Immigration Commission, *Reports,* XXIV, 830-31.

[36] See e.g., Oral History, Tad Tomita, March 23, 1984; "Tad Tomita: Strawberry Success Story," *Western Grower & Shipper,* 49:9 (September 1978), 6-7, 9; and *The Naturipe Story,* n.p., n.d.

[37] Immigration Commission, *Reports,* XXIV, 830-31.

[38] Oral History, John Hayakawa, March 8, 1984.

[39] Oral History, Katsusaburo Kawahara, January 25, 1984.

[40] Oral History, John Hayakawa, March 8, 1984.

[41] Oral History, Henry Kurasaki, February 23, 1984.

[42] Oral History, Kaoru Inouye, August 22, 1984; and letter, Kaoru Inouye to Gary Okihiro, May 27, 1984.

[43] Oral History, Kazuto Nakamura, March 13, 1984.

[44] Oral History, Phil Y. Matsumura, February 16 and 23, 1984.

[45] Oral History, Satoru Kawashima, January 12, 1984; Oral History, Harry Araki, March 13, 1984; and Oral History, Katsusaburo Kawahara, February 8, 1984.

[46] Oral History, Phil Y. Matsumura, February 16, 1984.

[47] Oral History, Eiichi Sakauye, May 4, 1983; Oral History, Yoshio Ando, November 11, 1983; Oral History, Katsusaburo Kawahara, February 8, 1984; and Bloom and Reimer, *Removal and Return,* 83-96.

[48] Immigration Commission, *Reports,* XXIV, 450-51.

[49] See, e.g., Noritaka Yagasaki, "Ethnic Cooperativism and Immigrant Agriculture: A Study of Japanese Floriculture and Truck Farming in California," unpubl. Ph.D. dissertation, University of California, Berkeley, 1982.

[50] Oral History, Yoshio Ando, November 11, 1983.

[51] Gunki Kai, "Economic Status of the Japanese in California," unpubl. M.A. thesis, Stanford University, 1920, 61.

[52] Oral History, Satoru Kawashima, January 12, 1984.

[53] Oral History, Eiichi Sakauye, May 4, 1983.

[54] Takeda, "Autobiography," 6.

[55] Takeda, "Autobiography," 8.

[56] Oral History, Shoji Takeda, December 21, 1983.

[57] Takeda, "Autobiography," 9.

[58] Oral History, Shoji Takeda, December 21, 1983.

[59] Takeda, "Autobiography," 21.

[60] Oral History, Shoji Takeda, December 29, 1983.

[61] Takeda, "Autobiography," 21-22.

[62] Oral History, Yoshio Ando, November 11, 1983.

[63] Oral History, Shoji Takeda, December 29, 1983.

[64] The Santa Clara County Pea Growers Company, started by Japanese farmers around 1930, also marketed their produce in the East Coast through a broker in San Jose. The company was essentially a marketing cooperative with a paid manager, Okagaki, and a packing shed on 27th Street. Oral History, Shoji Takeda, December 29, 1983.

[65] Oral History, Yoshio Ando, January 19, 1984.

[66] Oral History, Yoshio Ando, January 19, 1984; and Oral History, Shoji Takeda, December 29, 1983.

[67] Oral History, Yoshio Ando, October 26, 1983.

[68] *California and the Oriental,* Report of the State Board of Control of California, June 19, 1920, Sacramento, 1922, 50.

[69] Sawyer, *History of Santa Clara County,* 139.

[70] *San Jose Mercury,* October 15 and 23, 1920; Fowler, "Some Aspects of Public Opinion," 102-03; and David C. Drummond, "An Account of Japanese Agriculture in Santa Clara County During the 1920's: A Methodological Exercise," unpubl. seminar paper, University of Santa Clara, 1983, 16.

[71] File titled, "Divorce Cases, 1900-53," Japanese Farming in the Santa Clara Valley Project, University of Santa Clara.

[72] Oral History, Shoji Takeda, December 21, 1983; and Oral History, John Hayakawa, March 8, 1984.

[73] Takeda, "Autobiography," 14-15; and Oral History, Shoji Takeda, December 21, 1983.

Nadeshiko
PINK

CHAPTER 6
MIGRANT LABORERS ONCE AGAIN

On the eve of World War II, Japanese farmers in the Santa Clara Valley were making some progress. In fact, they were on the verge of what might have become an economic take-off. They had survived the exceedingly difficult Depression years through forming cooperatives and, as in the initial period of Japanese tenancy, through wage labor. The latter strategy was especially prevalent during the winter months when farm incomes were particularly low. Others worked longer hours, cultivated larger acreages, and diversified their crops following shifts in the market. Orchardists like the Kurasakis pulled out their prune trees and planted raspberries and strawberries because these fetched higher prices.[1] On the whole, Japanese farmers had recovered from the Depression doldrums by 1940 and, despite the constraints of dependency, were beginning to move toward self-sufficiency.

According to the 1940 census, there were 390 Japanese farm operators in Santa Clara County. Most of these (165) were clustered in the San Jose area, while Santa Clara held 56, and Gilroy, 43.[2] Japanese farmers had made significant inroads into farm ownership; about 22 percent of all Japanese farm operators in the county were landowners. Land ownership was clearly an advance over farm tenancy and constituted the mandatory basis for economic self-determination.

Further evidence of the maturity of the Japanese American community as a whole is seen in the changes undergone in San Jose's Nihonmachi. During the first decade of the twentieth century, Nihonmachi was a servant of the surrounding farms in the valley. Boardinghouses and allied businesses dominated the life of the town, reflecting the reason for its existence — its function as a labor reserve. In 1940, Nihonmachi, like the farming clusters that developed during the intervening decades, was a community of homes and businesses catering to the needs of families. For example, on Jackson, Fifth, and Sixth Streets, there were 26 residences, 3 confectionary stores, 3 restaurants, 3 dry goods/general merchandise stores, 3 insurance agents, 2 markets, 2 physicians, 2 barbershops, 2 gas stations, and a tailor, a dressmaker, a watch repair store, a photographer, a fish market, a soda works, a furniture store, a pharmacy, a printer, a stationery store, and a laundry in addition to other businesses. There were also the Buddhist and Methodist churches, the office of the Japanese Association, and the Japanese language school. The only reminders of the period of migrant labor were a solitary hotel and a billiard parlor.[3]

Unchanged, nonetheless, was the fact that agriculture was the principal form of livelihood. The 1940 census listed 1,152 Japanese Americans as being employed in the county. Of these, 882 were employed in agriculture, 120 in personal service, 75 in the wholesale and retail business, 18 in manufacturing, and 57 in other areas.[4] These Japanese farmers were approaching the new decade with expectations of comparative prosperity. Katsusaburo Kawahara leased 40 acres from J.J. O'Brien on Brokaw Road in 1921. In 1927, he expanded to 80 acres, then to 150 acres, and by World War II, he leased 225 acres. Kawahara hired several Japanese families during the 1930s to help with the farm work, and after 1935, hired up to ten Filipino men during the harvest season.[5] In 1937, Kaso Hayakawa rented 13 acres in the Trimble Road area and grew raspberries and blackberries. Beginning the following year and continuing up to World War II, Hayakawa switched to row crops including celery, cucumbers, and stringbeans. The December 1941 celery harvest was particularly good. The Hayakawas worked long hours and were making about $100 per day, a considerable amount. The outlook appeared rosy.[6] In 1936, the Ezaki family purchased 14.5 acres in Alviso, and in 1941, added 13.5 acres to their property.[7] Yoshio Ando purchased 46 acres on North First Street in 1937. He grew mainly celery, bell peppers, and cauliflower, and employed three or four Filipinos and a few Mexicans to work the land. But that was before the war.

Exclusionism (Expulsion) and Dependency

December 7, 1941, marked a turning point in the lives of Japanese farmers in the valley, indeed in the United States. Not because of what they did, but because of what was done to them. On the one hand, the war offered the opportunity for immediate gains through the expropriation of Japanese farm properties and crops, while on the other, it posed a problem for the government in maintaining food production and for landlords and canners who profited from Japanese farmers. Thus counterpoised were the interests of exclusionism (expulsion) and dependency, accounting for the

seemingly contradictory responses of the valley's elites. While warning of "enemies within our gates," the *Mercury Herald* editorial of February 14, 1942, counseled against vigilante remedies: "The regularly constituted police forces are well qualified to take care of the situation in an orderly and legal manner. Should they require additional assistance there are thousands of special police already sworn in and under training."[8] Even after Executive Order 9066, the *Mercury Herald,* in an editorial on February 25, 1942, showed remarkable equanimity:

It should not need the informed word of Tom C. Clark, coordinator of enemy alien control, to convince Washington that a custodian is immediately needed for the property of 8067 enemy alien families on this coast as they are moved inland. It is a provision that should have been made before this time. Sudden shifts of population raise many problems even where the physical job is not complicated by emotional factors. Many of these families must move before they can provide adequate care for their property. There will be persons who capitalize upon their necessities. There may even be thoughtless [sic] who so far forget their Americanism to commit outrages against these properties at times when bad war news stirs up fruitless hates.

It could be said that such excesses are not American. They are not even adult. They are about on a par with the pettiness of a person who kicks a chair because he has stubbed his toe on it in the dark. Sensible control of these properties by a properly constituted governmental agency will protect both the properties and our emotions from childish and pointless excesses.

The Hayes brothers, owners of the *Mercury Herald*, were responding to anti-Japanese exclusionists like local Congressman John Z. Anderson who was a leader in urging the mass removal (expulsion) of Japanese from the West Coast, and to incidences of vandalism and violence directed against Japanese American property in the area. On December 12, 1941, the *Mercury Herald* reported that on the previous night, during a blackout in Santa Cruz County, "several trees on the high cliff in an area inhabited by Japanese strawberry growers suddenly began burning." On February 27, 1942, a "fire of mysterious origin" gutted the basement of the Japanese Buddhist temple on North Fifth Street. According to the Reverend Aso, the room was padlocked every night by the caretaker, but firemen reported they found the padlock open and several matches on the floor.[9]

In their response to the exclusionists, E.A. and J.O. Hayes revealed their true concern — the maintenance of Japanese dependency. Their editorial, urging the protection of alien property, was not unlike Sheriff John Murphy's defense of the Chabolla family in the "Settlers War of 1861." Both rose in defense of private property — the underpinning of American capitalism — and both were motivated by self-interest.

That reading of the *Mercury Herald* is made clear in the month of March. On the front page of its March 6, 1942 edition, under the by-line, "No Jap Evacuation Here — Yet," the paper reported that Lt. General John L. DeWitt, commander in charge of the defense of the West Coast, did not contemplate the removal of Japanese from the Santa Clara Valley until after steps had been taken to provide for their property rights. That plan was reinforced by local Sheriff William J. Emig, the report continued, who believed that the Japanese would not be evicted for at least sixty days to allow time for them to plant their crops. The valley's agricultural interest groups were worried, concluded the report, because "nearly 7,000 acres are planted by aliens here," and Emig estimated that for the year, the tomato crop alone would be worth "close to a million dollars." Three days later, the *Mercury Herald* reported that the number of acres of agricultural land under Japanese operation "increased nearly 30 percent from 1939 1940." Japanese dependency was indeed profitable.

Exclusionism Effected

Meanwhile, on March 2, DeWitt established Military Areas No. 1 and 2. The former included roughly the western half of the states of Washington, Oregon, and California and the southern half of Arizona, while the latter consisted of the remaining portions of those four states. Restrictions were placed on enemy aliens and "voluntary evacuation" was encouraged. The Santa Clara Valley fell within Military Area No. 1, and many Japanese families, thinking that moving to Military Area No. 2 would spare them the eventuality of forced eviction, left the valley for the interior. The family of Shoji Takeda, for example, moved to Gridley in Butte County in Military Area No. 2, and farmed canning tomatoes for the James Mills Corporation.[10] Others, like the family of

Yoshio Ando, managed to leave California and thereby avoid the wholesale removal and confinement of Japanese in Military Areas No. 1 and 2.[11] "Voluntary evacuation" ended with DeWitt's order on March 29, forcing those who remained in the Santa Clara Valley to await the anticipated eviction under the direction of the U.S. Army.

The Wartime Civil Control Administration (WCCA) appealed to Japanese farmers to continue producing food as a demonstration of their loyalty, and, at the same time, attempted to transfer Japanese farms to non-Japanese operators. That process, under way in the Santa Clara Valley, was reported in the *Mercury Herald* of March 6, 1942, when the U.S. Department of Agriculture in the county was instructed to advise Japanese, Italian, and German farmers that "they may best demonstrate their loyalty to the United States by continuing their present operations and making certain that growing crops are not lost through sabotage or neglect." The "advice" was in reality a threat. On April 2, 1942, under the heading, "Tenants for Lands Vacated by Japanese Sought by WCCA Here," the *Mercury Herald* reported that according to the WCCA, several thousands of acres of vegetables, berries, and sugarbeets were being left uncultivated by Japanese farmers, and white growers were reluctant to take over the operation of berry land. A prospective tenant offered to plow the Japanese-planted crops under and raise his own produce but was reminded of the Army's warning that any person, Japanese or non-Japanese, who destroyed crops would be dealt with as a saboteur.

To Japanese farmers, the meaning of that threat was consistent with their historical experience. Their continued presence in America was predicated on their usefulness, first as migrant laborers and later as dependent communities. Uninterrupted farm production while awaiting expulsion and confinement was clearly exploitative of Japanese labor. Further, the government was grossly hypocritical in framing that exploitation as a proof of Japanese American loyalty. Finally, in anticipation of the mass removal of Japanese from the valley, the government turned to a familiar solution to its labor problem. On April 17, the Farm Security Administration announced that San Francisco Chinese were arranging to take over the 190 Japanese farms not yet transferred. Lawrence Lee of Victory Farms Company wrote that the company's chief desire was "to help Uncle Sam produce the food he needs" and was prepared to send Chinese farm laborers including "hard working Chinese women."[12] This scheme may have inspired the War Relocation Authority, the WCCA's civilian successor, to sponsor the recruitment of Chinese agricultural labor from San Francisco to replace the Japanese in the central valleys later that same year. In any case, the transfer of Japanese farms without interrupting production served the purposes of both the exclusionists like Congressman Anderson and those who profited from Japanese dependency. Paraphrasing the *Mercury Herald* editorial, "sensible control" of Japanese properties had indeed protected the valley from un-American "excesses."

Unfortunately for Japanese farmers, while their properties were being "safeguarded," their best interests were not being served. The Farm Security Administration reported on April 17 that all but 190 of the 580 Japanese farms registered with that agency in the county had been taken over by non-

Japanese operators.[13] The transfer of Japanese farms in the valley, however, was frequently effected without bureaucratic assistance. Individual farmers made their own arrangements in the hopes that the recipients, friends or persons recommended by friends, could be entrusted with the faithful upkeep of the property. Yoshio Ando rented his farm to former Filipino employee, Johnny Ibarra, for a nominal amount that simply covered the taxes and mortgage interest on the land.[14] Katsusaburo Kawahara, a cash tenant holding over 200 acres, was approached by a former schoolmate, Leo Garcillo, and asked to sell his crops and farm equipment to Garcillo and his partner, Al Gomes. The two paid $3,000 for the entire operation including crops, tractors, greenhouses, and other farm implements.[15]

On May 21, 1942, the *Mercury Herald* reported that the WCCA warned all Japanese in northern Santa Clara County "to close their affairs promptly and make their own arrangements for disposal of personal and real property." Japanese Americans were instructed to deposit their cars with the WCCA office at 280 South Market Street, and, the report announced, "Persons interested in purchasing one of these cars or trucks can see a list of them by calling at the office." The same issue of the *Mercury,* under the eye-catching (for an agricultural county) heading, "Japs To Work Oregon Farms," noted that DeWitt had approved a plan for 200 Japanese to leave the Portland assembly center to work on the sugar beet farms of eastern Oregon where there was a farm labor shortage. Two days later, the paper repeated the story, adding that the Japanese would work "chiefly in 'thinning' the rows through their accustomed 'stoop labor.'"

On Sunday and Monday, May 24 and 25, Japanese living in the county registered with the WCCA control station set up in the men's gymnasium at San Jose State College. In all, 2,847 registered.[16] Special trains, one per day from Tuesday, May 26, through Friday, May 29, departed from the Southern Pacific station on North San Pedro Street. Their destination was Santa Anita racetrack, described by the reporter as "the spacious race track near Los Angeles... equipped as a reception center."[17] Army military police secured the area around the train station; other military police rode the trains. The *Mercury Herald* of May 27 offered a poignant description of the scene at the train station:

> The evacuees were orderly and appeared to be in good spirits. Most of them conversed among themselves in English. In the waiting lines were mothers with babes in their arms alongside elderly Japanese, some of whom said they had been here 40 years, also, nattily dressed younger women carrying the latest slick magazine to read on the trip.
>
> Among them passed a group of women from the First Presbyterian church, offering hot coffee to the adults, milk to the children. In the crowd, too, were American women who had gone to the station to say goodbye to Japanese friends and wish them well.

Two photographs accompanied the May 30 report on the "evacuation finale." The first pictured members of the San Jose Boy Scout Troop No. 38, helping to carry the baggage of fellow Japanese Americans as they boarded the train. The Boy

Scouts, the article read, "seized the opportunity yesterday to do their good deed for the day even under the stress of being evacuated." The second photograph showed white women from the First Presbyterian church and Mrs. Joseph Cooper of San Jose State College YWCA handing out fruit, milk, and coffee to the last group of Japanese Americans to leave the county.

Exclusionism Enshrined

The deed was done. The community had been purged of the "yellow peril" and had achieved a greater measure of homogeneity. However, ridding the county of Japanese Americans was not enough for the exclusionists. They sought to make that absence permanent. Nearly a year after the forced removal of Japanese Americans from the valley, on May 8, 1943, the Morgan Hill city council voiced its unanimous opposition to the resettlement of Japanese Americans there. The city, the *Mercury Herald* of May 9 reported, "is opposed to the relocation of Japanese and...no Japanese laborers are wanted here." The following month, on June 14, both the San Jose city council and the Santa Clara County board of supervisors voted to oppose the return of Japanese Americans to the West Coast for the duration of the war.[18] During the deliberations, councilmember Earl C. Campbell stated his desire for the valley's Japanese Americans: "I personally hope that the Japanese in this county will be more dispersed and that we will no longer have a Japanese problem." Thus, according to Campbell and the Morgan Hill city council in 1943, the "Japanese problem" was not one of labor, but of community.

Most of the county's Japanese Americans were confined at Heart Mountain concentration camp in Wyoming until 1945. Meanwhile, in the Santa Clara Valley, the temporary void left by their departure was quickly filled by white ethnics and people of color. Italian and Portuguese growers moved into truck farming, especially profitable during the war, and Filipinos, Mexicans, and Blacks provided for the labor needs of the valley's orchards and fields and the rapidly growing war industries. Illustrative of that substitution was San Jose's Nihonmachi, which soon housed mainly Filipinos and Blacks,[19] and the Orchard School, which enrolled primarily children with Spanish surnames. Japanese farmers, thus, were hardly missed. In fact, the war transformed the valley's economy, making the pre-war Japanese farming community obsolete.

Despite the predominance of agriculture, the 1940s witnessed fundamental changes in the valley's political economy. The booming wartime industries in the northern counties of Contra Costa, Alameda, and San Mateo were eventually attracted to Santa Clara County. A concerted public relations campaign and the combination of plenty of cheap land, weak unions, and financial incentives helped to stimulate industrial and urban growth.[20] What followed, of course, was the transformation of the valley into our present-day sprawling metropolis and a haven for high-technology. Although that transformation properly belongs to the decades of the 1950s and 1960s, the groundwork was laid during the 1930s and 1940s.[21] A major consequence for agriculture was the soaring land value — a situation that choked and eventually killed off the valley's gardens and orchards.

The Exiles Return

On December 17, 1944, General Henry Pratt, DeWitt's replacement and head of the Western Defense Command, issued a press release stating that, "Those persons of Japanese ancestry whose records have stood the test of Army scrutiny during the past two years," would be released from confinement after January 2, 1945, and would be "permitted the same freedom of movement throughout the United States as other loyal citizens and law-abiding aliens."[22] The Army maintained three classes of Japanese Americans: the first, on the "cleared list," were those that military intelligence deemed "suitable to locate wherever they choose"; the second category, termed "exclude," were those who could move anywhere except to their places of origin; and the third class, "detained for having caused trouble," were mainly those Japanese Americans classified as "disloyal" and kept in confinement at Tule Lake concentration camp.[23]

Gradually, the exiles returned. The *Mercury Herald* of January 4, 1945, announced "Jap Woman Takes Palo Alto Job." The report noted the lifting of the exclusion orders, and named a Mrs. Morowaki and her two-year old daughter as being the first to leave the Topaz concentration camp. Permission was granted because she was the wife of an "American soldier." Soon, other Japanese Americans returned to the valley. On March 9, the War Relocation Authority (WRA) established an office in San Jose, headed by a former newspaperman, James E. Edmiston, to assist the resettlement of the returning Japanese Americans. Edmiston and the WRA staff helped to find housing and employment for the Japanese, and investigated charges of discrimination and harassment directed against them.

While helpful, the government's provision for Japanese resettlement was meager when compared with the magnitude of the losses sustained under government-sponsored removal and confinement. Japanese farmers, like all Japanese Americans displaced during the war, were faced with the prospect of starting all over again. Economic losses were enormous, frequently total. An Issei farmer testified shortly after the war:

> Before war I had 20 acres in Berryessa. Good land, two good houses, one big. 1942 in camp everybody say sell, sell, sell. Maybe lose all. Lawyer write, he say sell. I sell $650 acre. Now the same land $1500 acre. I lose, I cannot help. All gone. Now I live in hostel. Work like when first come to this country. Pick cherries, pick pears, pick apricots, pick tomatoes. Just like when first come. Pretty soon, maybe one year, maybe two years, find place. Pretty hard now. Now spend $15,000 just for [half as much] land. No good material for house. No get farm machinery. No use look back. Go crazy think about all lost. Have to start all over again like when come from Japan, but faster this time.[24]

Before the war, Sam Uchiyama and his brothers, Katsuzo and Shigaru, had been orchardists near Los Gatos:

> The three brothers had stored their families' belongings in a house they owned near Los Gatos. They had carefully boarded up the place with two-by-six planks. When he

returned to San Jose, Sam Uchiyama reported to WRA headquarters. Edmiston drove out with him to check on the Uchiyama family possessions. Not only were the household goods gone, but the house in which they had been stored was gone.

"People thought they'd seen the last of the Japanese forever," explained Edmiston. "It was open season and they took everything."

Dismayed at the loss, Uchiyama decided to return to the *evacue* camp and stay there, a ward of the government that had uprooted him.[25]

Other Japanese farmers returning to the valley discovered similar fates. Their homes and barns were ransacked, and frequently their fields were covered with weeds.[26] They, however, were fortunate in that they still had the land. Tenant farmers, the vast majority of Japanese farmers in the valley, were not as lucky. The WRA reported, "In the Santa Clara Valley...few whose prewar farm operations depended on leased land were able to resume farming. Owners, however, had no great difficulty in getting back their land. A very few managed to get land they leased before the war."[27] In some instances, even owners of farm property had trouble recovering their land. Yasuto Kato placed his farm under the care of a white operator who agreed to run it on a 70-30 share basis — 70 percent for himself and 30 percent for the Katos. During the war, the family received no money from the white operator, and he refused to make an accounting. "When Yasuto returned to the Santa Clara Valley to take over the family farm, the administrator was deep in a local 'Keep the Japs

out' agitation. Only after WRA officials cracked down on the administrator was Yasuto Kato... able to get their own property back and to plant crops."[28]

Even more horrendous was the experience of the Araki family, Japanese farmers who lost their farm property completely to an unscrupulous white operator. At the outbreak of World War II, Suyetaro Araki owned about 55 acres of the old Hostetter Ranch in Berryessa, and cash leased 60 acres on the Roach Ranch in Milpitas, about 50 acres of the Farney Ranch near Wayne Station, and 20 acres on the Hudson property across from his home ranch. As events began to look bleak for the Japanese, Suyetaro terminated his leases and sought to consolidate all of his holdings on his home ranch. His son Harry took a whole month collecting and taking an inventory of the gathered farm equipment. Before being removed, Harry arranged to have a white businessman, a trusted family friend, run the farm during their absence. Suyetaro died at Heart Mountain concentration camp in September 1942. When the Arakis returned in 1945, they learned that the farm no longer belonged to them. Apparently, during the war, the white manager had transferred the property title to his name. He refused to see or speak with Harry, and Harry was advised by an attorney that there was nothing that could be done. After suffering a nervous breakdown, Harry worked as a carpenter. His mother, Chiyo, was committed to Agnew State Hospital where she died in 1960.[29] These too were the casualties of America's concentration camps.

A "Happy State of Affairs"

Throughout the spring and summer of 1945,

they came to the Santa Clara Valley in trains from desolate places like Heart Mountain, Topaz, Poston, and Gila River. The WRA reported 60 Japanese Americans in the county in March, 600 in June, 2,500 in October, and nearly 7,000 in January 1946.[30] The total amounted to about twice the prewar Japanese American population in the county. That phenomenon has been cited as an indication of the relative absence of anti-Japanese hostility in the valley. "The Santa Clara Valley," wrote Taylor, "was one of the bright spots of tolerance in California's treatment of its exiles. Although looting and exploiting of property of the *evacues* were routine in the valley, as elsewhere in the Army's restricted area, violence and intimidation were at a minimum."[31] Zambetti, citing oral histories of local Japanese Americans concluded, "Here in Santa Clara County no such pressure was applied against the Japanese and because of this. . . three times as many Japanese returned to this area than were evacuated in 1942. Many came from the hostile climates of Monterey and San Joaquin Counties to find refuge here."[32]

Edmiston, head of the local WRA office, speaking before the San Jose Schoolmen's Club on the night of November 1, 1945, congratulated the residents of Santa Clara County for their cordial reception of returning Japanese Americans. "Nisei and their parents," he was quoted as saying, "returning to ordinary life from the relocation centers have been better received here than anywhere else."[33] On January 27, 1946, in a final report published in the *Mercury Herald,* Edmiston reflected, "We didn't expect the relocation process to go along quite as smoothly as it has. . . . The WRA can close shop on May 4 with the feeling that this is a difficult problem which Santa Clara County has opened its mind to and solved very well." The claim was not baseless. Edmiston pointed to the number of Japanese Americans settling in the county. Further, he stated, "The Japanese do not find themselves discriminated against in schools. In employment circles they are meeting minimum opposition. Most labor unions have agreed to accept them into their ranks."[34]

The realities of everyday life for Japanese Americans, however, contradicted Edmiston's summation. He himself was the object of anti-Japanese violence. A shot was fired through the window of his house, and he was nicknamed "Suzuki" because he was a "Jap-lover."[35] On March 6, assailants cut the telephone lines and set fire to the house of the family of Joe Takeda, pear ranchers on Alviso Road. When Takeda and his son rushed out to fight the blaze, shots were fired at them.[36] A barber chair was thrown through the glass window of Toshi Takeda's store on Jackson Street in Nihonmachi on the night of March 23, 1945.[37] The *Mercury* reported on April 7 that Elsie Inouye had filed charges of job discrimination against her former employer, the County Hospital. On April 10, arsonists were suspected of starting a fire in a building owned by T. Okida at 610 North Fifth Street,[38] and on May 12, the *Mercury* reported that vandals broke into the San Jose Buddhist temple on North Fifth Street and damaged property stored there by 21 Japanese families. "Youths Suspected in Nip Temple Raid," the by-line read. On May 19, the *Mercury* noted that Harry Dobashi, a former merchant in Nihonmachi, had been refused employment at the California Packing Corporation cannery. As a result, the

San Jose WRA office was instructed by the War Manpower Commission to begin "an intense educational campaign" to break down prejudice against Japanese Americans. Calpack, the report concluded, had no objections to hiring Japanese Americans "provided that the 'educational campaign' changed the attitude of other employes [sic]."

Surely those attitudes and behaviors, although considered "excesses" by the dominant class, were more in line with the pre-war anti-Japanese movement than with Edmiston's roseate portrayal. In addition, the daily terrors of possible violence against one's self and family and racism in the workplace almost certainly impeded the full pursuit of life, liberty, and property. Despite the comparative infrequency of that oppression, it functioned much like the unenforced alien land laws in establishing white supremacy. Those "excesses" reminded Japanese Americans of "their place," and they buttressed the prevailing social relations. A WRA report offered an explanation for the "hospitality" extended to returning Japanese Americans in the valley. Prejudice was exhibited to a lesser degree in the county, the report observed, because the Japanese were not in direct economic competition with whites.[39]

Edmiston, when assessing the reasons for the county's claimed receptivity, was reported to have said, "He credited democratic teaching in the County's schools and willingness of the American-Japanese to work hard this Autumn in saving the endangered fruit crop as being the main reason for the happy state of affairs here."[40] Since instruction in American democracy was certainly not restricted to Santa Clara County, this statement does little to

explain the valley's apparently exemplary behavior vis-a-vis other counties in the state. Rather, the truth, we believe, is contained in Edmiston's candid appraisal of the role of Japanese American labor. In June, July, and August of 1945, the *Mercury* reported a notable shortage of agricultural labor in the county.[41] Taylor wrote: "Edmiston's job of settling the Japanese-Americans on farms was greatly eased after V-J Day when gasoline restrictions were lifted. The Mexicans and Okies who had been the war-time farm workers gassed up and hit the highways, leaving the prune crop lying on the ground. An outcry came from farmers to save the fruit. The Japanese moved in and saved the crop."[42] Just as valley residents had in 1942 supported a late removal of the Japanese in order that the crops might first be planted, so was the harvest of the 1945 crop in jeopardy, and was in fact saved by the returning Japanese laborers. The icy terrors directed against Japanese Americans during the winter and spring melted in the heat of the summer's harvest.

Migrant Laborers Once Again

The first large contingent of Japanese Americans to return to the valley arrived on June 7, 1945. The group, internees from Heart Mountain, numbered about 100, and included mainly women and children joining their husbands who had preceded them. Most were farm families. "Some of the group's family heads own ranches," the report noted, "others live on leased ranches and some are ranch workers."[43] The local WRA office, besides assisting in locating housing, received requests for Japanese labor. In the early spring, jobs included farm labor, work in industry, and domestic work.[44]

By summer, the demand for Japanese agricultural labor far exceeded all other kinds of employment opportunities. In October, "According to Edmiston, 95 percent of the returning Japanese-Americans have been relocated on ranches. For that reason, he has been unable to meet requests for them for household employment in town."[45] In January of the following year, when there were about twice as many Japanese Americans in the valley as before the war, Edmiston reported that the WRA office had "a request for 100 farm workers which it cannot fill."[46]

Long forgotten were the 1943 resolutions of the city councils of San Jose and Morgan Hill, and the Santa Clara County board of supervisors for the exclusion of Japanese Americans from the valley. Pragmatic economic concerns once again outweighed political posturing. One of the largest employers of Japanese farm labor was the Driscoll brothers property in the vicinity of Morgan Hill.[47] The influx of Japanese in the fall of 1945 caused a minor crisis for the schools in that town because of overcrowding, but the problem was solved at the Burnette School by having a room fixed to accommodate the Japanese American children and by hiring a new teacher. The pupils who merited that concern by Morgan Hill in 1945 were the children of Japanese American families who had been hired to pick 150 acres of strawberries on the Driscoll property.[48] Other landowners in the valley similarly welcomed the returning Japanese American farmers — potential tenants. A Nisei recalled: "He [landowner] was really glad to see me. He had been having an awful time trying to run the place himself with the kind of labor he could get during the war. First thing he wanted to know if I could come back and take over the place so that he wouldn't have to think of it anymore."[49]

Japanese American growers who were able to recover their farms were inundated with Japanese American labor. Many of these were family friends who simply needed a place to stay and temporary employment until they could get started on their own again. Yoshio Ando hired four or five Japanese families, built new quarters for them, and had them work on his farm. Most of these left after about a year to become sharecroppers or enter into other work.[50] Shoji Takeda hired many Japanese families after the war including the Abe, Idehara, Kikuchi, Kiyohara, Kusumoto, Matsui, Nagasaki, Nakashima, Oyama, and Sasaki families. Many of these were highly skilled farmers who helped a great deal in running the Takeda farm. Although they were wage workers, they actually assisted in managing the farm,[51] and the relationship was mutually beneficial. Recalled Takeda:

There were many displaced families who lost everything during the war and had no place to return to. Therefore, we took the opportunity to help them as well as to help solve some of our problems for the interim until they may find an occupation of their choosing. We began receiving letters from friends in camp who had decided to stay incarcerated because they had no place to go and now must decide where to relocate to. Many of those individuals were farmers in their own right but had lost everything or worse on sharecrop basis [sic] before departure. Therefore, we were willing to house the families in all of the available houses on our farm. Also, some of the families found homes in town and elsewhere but did not have any employment so we gave them employment until they would decide for themselves what they would like to do or sought other employment. This gave us an opportunity to farm celery once again and also gave others an opportunity to become organized with some sort of income. . . .[52]

A good number of the returning Japanese farmers planted strawberries in the summer and fall of 1945. Yoshio Ando remembered his reluctance to grow strawberries but went ahead anyway and planted three acres. The reason for his mixed feelings about strawberries was the crop required intensive care and labor, but it yielded fruit after only three months and the post-war prices were very good.[53] Strawberries, thus, gave Japanese farmers in the valley their start both in the earliest farm settlement in Alviso and in the rebirth of the community after World War II.

Starting over, however, was never quite the same. The nature of farming in the valley had been transformed during the war, and Japanese farmers themselves had changed. Although twice the number of Japanese returned to the valley as were there before the war, many came as migrant laborers seeking employment opportunities and left when those had been exhausted. Edmiston reported that although the valley's hospitality drew Japanese Americans who were not former residents of the county, "the newcomers are leaving again as rapidly as possible for their former places of residence."[54]

Zambetti, again relying on oral histories, described the attitude of returning farmers.

But this renewed activity of the Japanese in farming was of a different hue than the earlier involvement of the first immigrants. These newer farmers were not looking forward to life on the farm, these people had other ambitions and sought other means of support. Gradually many became gardeners and others went into nursery and floral businesses.[55]

Perhaps they had vivid memories of the difficult pre-war years, or perhaps they recognized the restructured political economy and the futility of garden farming. It was crystal clear, however, that for the vast majority of Japanese farmers, their days were numbered and farming no longer offered any possibility of economic self-sufficiency. During the war, they had been uprooted like weeds and left to dry in the desert sun. They had been rendered innocuous and had even become irrelevant to the interests of capital. They were relics of a by-gone past, made obsolete by industry, high-technology, astronomical land prices, freeways, and suburbia. They were, like Urashima Taro, strangers in their own land. In the words of the Issei farmer quoted previously, "All gone. Now I live in hostel."

Internees probably leaving Heart Mountain Camp. Japanese Americans began returning to the Santa Clara Valley from Heart Mountain in January of 1945.
Courtesy of Misaye Santo.

Riichi Nishimura family, tenant farmers in Los Gatos, with their packed belongings leaving for internment in May 1942. The family landlord is shaking hands with Riichi.
Courtesy of Hideko Morishita.

Santa Clara Valley Japanese opened up what was a dry and unproductive region of Heart Mountain, Wyoming, to agriculture. They brought in a variety of vegetable crops to show the agricultural potential of the region.
Courtesy of the Sakauye Family, California History Center Archives.

Harvesting tomatoes at Heart Mountain concentration camp. Japanese farmers, although confined, continued to produce for the benefit of the community.

Obon at Heart Mountain concentration camp in 1943. Displays of Japanese culture during the wartime period were remarkable testimonies to the perseverance of the people especially since Japanese language and culture were viewed as being anti-American.
Courtesy of Misaye Santo.

George Santo standing in front of the Old Santo Market on Jackson Street in San Jose Nihonmachi. The photograph was taken shortly after the war. Note the American products being sold in contrast with Japanese markets just three decades earlier.
Courtesy of Misaye Santo.

Japanese delegation planting cherry trees at the Gilroy Hot Springs, c.1935. The famous Hot Springs was purchased by H.K. Sakata in 1935. The resort was vacated during World War II but reopened after the war as a hostel for the returning Japanese families. In the 1950s, modernization of the pool facilities and the planting of a beautiful bamboo grove resulted in its renewed popularity.
California History Center Archives.

Footnotes

[1] Oral History, Henry Kurasaki, February 23, 1984.

[2] Wartime Civil Control Administration, Statistical Section, *Bulletin No. 6,* April 11, 1942, 3.

[3] Hirabayashi, "San Jose Nihonmachi," 43-50.

[4] Wartime Civil Control Administration, Statistical Section, *Bulletin No. 7,* April 13, 1942. According to the Wartime Civil Control Administration, Statistical Section, *Bulletin No. 10,* May 15, 1942, there were 454 farmers and farm managers, 315 farm laborers (wage earners), and 383 farm laborers (unpaid family members) in the county.

[5] Oral History, Katsusaburo Kawahara, January 25, 1984, and February 8, 1984.

[6] Oral History, John Hayakawa, February 24, 1984, and March 2, 1984.

[7] Oral History, Tom Ezaki, January 27, 1984, and February 2, 1984.

[8] See also *San Jose Mercury Herald* editorials of January 30, 1942, and February 4, 1942.

[9] *San Jose Mercury Herald,* February 28, 1942.

[10] Takeda, "Autobiography," 33-40.

[11] Oral History, Yoshio Ando, November 2, 1983.

[12] *San Jose Mercury Herald,* April 17, 1942.

[13] *San Jose Mercury Herald,* April 17, 1942.

[14] Oral History, Yoshio Ando, November 2, 1983.

[15] Oral History, Katsusaburo Kawahara, February 8, 1984.

[16] *San Jose Mercury Herald,* May 24 and 26, 1942.

[17] *San Jose Mercury Herald,* May 25, 1942.

[18] *San Jose Mercury Herald,* June 15, 1943.

[19] Girdner and Loftis, *Great Betrayal,* 408.

[20] Mitchell Mandich, "The Growth and Development of San Jose, California — Social, Political, and Economic Considerations," unpubl. M.A. thesis, San Jose State University, 1975, 41-46.

[21] Mandich, "Growth and Development," 36-39.

[22] Quoted in Peter Irons, *Justice At War,*

Oxford University Press: New York, 1983, 345.

[23] *San Jose Mercury Herald,* March 15, 1945.

[24] War Relocation Authority, *People in Motion,* Government Printing Office: Washington, D.C., 1947, 53.

[25] Frank J. Taylor, "Home Again," *Collier's,* February 15, 1947, 35.

[26] See, e.g., Oral History, Yoshio Ando, November 11, 1983.

[27] WRA, *People in Motion,* 65.

[28] Taylor, "Home Again," 35. See also, Robert Zambetti, "The Japanese in Santa Clara County, 1940-1950," a paper presented to the Santa Clara County Pioneers Association, June 3, 1967, 10-11.

[29] Oral History, Harry Araki, March 13 and 20, 1984.

[30] *San Jose Mercury Herald,* March 15, 1945, June 8, 1945, October 3, 1945, and January 27, 1946.

[31] Taylor, "Home Again," 15, 34. See also, WRA, *People in Motion,* 65; and Dillon S. Myer, *Uprooted Americans,* University of Arizona Press: Tucson, 1971, 256.

[32] Zambetti, "Japanese in Santa Clara County," 12.

[33] *San Jose Mercury Herald,* November 2, 1945.

[34] *San Jose Mercury Herald,* January 27, 1946.

[35] Taylor, "Home Again," 34.

[36] *San Jose Mercury Herald,* March 7, 1945; and Taylor, "Home Again," 34.

[37] *San Jose Mercury Herald,* March 24, 1945.

[38] *San Jose Mercury Herald,* April 11 and 13, 1945.

[39] WRA, *People in Motion,* 61. See also, Zambetti, "Japanese in Santa Clara County," 12-13.

[40] *San Jose Mercury Herald,* November 2, 1945.

[41] *San Jose Mercury Herald,* June 8 and 12, 1945, July 14 and 15, 1945, and August 10, 1945.

[42] Taylor, "Home Again," 36.

[43] *San Jose Mercury Herald,* June 8, 1945.

[44] *San Jose Mercury Herald,* March 15, 1945.

[45] *San Jose Mercury Herald,* October 3, 1945.

[46] *San Jose Mercury Herald,* January 27, 1946.

[47] Oral History, Eiichi Sakauye, May 4, 1983.

[48] *San Jose Mercury Herald,* October 18 and 28, 1945, and November 3, 1945.

[49] Quoted in WRA, *People in Motion,* 65-66.

[50] Oral History, Yoshio Ando, November 11, 1983.

[51] Oral History, Shoji Takeda, December 29, 1983.

[52] Takeda, "Autobiography," 68-69.

[53] Oral History, Yoshio Ando, November 11, 1983. See also, Zambetti, "Japanese in Santa Clara County," 13-14.

[54] *San Jose Mercury Herald,* October 3, 1945.

[55] Zambetti, "Japanese in Santa Clara County," 14.

Ume
PLUM

CHAPTER 7
EPILOGUE:
OPPRESSION AND RESISTANCE

The return to migrant labor brings full circle our story of the experience of Japanese farmers in California's Santa Clara Valley. As the first Japanese in the valley disembarked from the barge at the landing at Alviso, they were greeted by white landowners with offers of work in their orchards. Sixty years later, as they stepped from the train at the station in Santa Clara, the homecoming Japanese were flooded with requests for their domestic and agricultural labor. Despite the apparent similarity, for the Issei the differences were deep and fundamental. When they first arrived in the valley as migrant laborers, they were young, strong, eagerly anticipating the sojourn. When they returned, they were advanced in years, sapped of their strength, measured in their step. The valley's landscape also had changed. They could not simply begin again.

The circuit, nonetheless, is consistent with our perspective on Japanese American history, and with our principal theme of struggle, of oppression and resistance. It also illustrates the cruel irony of the "model minority" stereotype. Our journey began with American merchant capital in 1784 when the *Empress of China* left New York harbor with its cargo of ginseng. American imperialism during the nineteenth century spread throughout the Pacific seeking raw materials and commodities, markets, and cheap labor. Asian workers were transported to Hawaii and the West Coast by way of the currents charted by those flows of capital and labor.

Thus around 1895, Japanese migrant laborers were similarly drawn to the Santa Clara Valley, and gradually replaced their Chinese predecessors. The work force was divided on the basis of color and ethnicity, as evidenced in the differential wages paid to whites, Chinese, and Japanese, and by task segregation, which reserved skilled positions for whites and unskilled work for Asians. Those tactics of the dominant class point to the exploitative nature of migrant labor and to the landowners' attempts to reduce the likelihood of collective resistance by the workers.

The labor shortage following the Gentlemen's Agreement of 1907 and Japanese resistance through strikes and threats of strikes resulted in higher wages and enabled the move into farm tenancy. Japanese "bosses" were in a better position to make that transition to tenancy than their "gang" members probably because they were able to accumulate capital at the expense of the workers. Further, they solved the labor problems of the white landowners, both in terms of securing workers and minimizing discontent. The alliance, then, of Japanese bosses and white landowners revealed an alignment of class interests, and marked the end of the period of migrant labor and the beginning of the period of dependency.

Japanese dependency was compelled not only by Japanese resistance, but also by the advance of capitalism in California agriculture. While the Chinese first labored under a paternalistic order, the Japanese entered during its breakup. This paternalism was evident in the Santa Clara Valley when the Chinese arrived during the early American phase dominated by immense ranches and a landed aristocracy. By 1880, the number of Chinese farm workers had swelled from 104 in 1870 to 689, and they constituted about 48 percent of the agricultural laborers in the county.[1] Besides that dangerous reliance by the growers on a monocultural work force, the Chinese showed indications of intractable behavior. The *San Francisco Bulletin* of August 18, 1880, reported a strike of Chinese fruitpickers in the Santa Clara Valley. The vehemently anti-Chinese movement in the valley, thus, was not circumstantial, but based on the economic stakes. Accompanying those labor trends were rising land values, the splitting of large landholdings, the infusion of capital, and the changeover from grains to orchards. Japanese migrants arrived in the valley during that transition, diversifying the agricultural work force and making farm tenancy profitable for the white landowners. Accordingly, when the Chinese work force reached a critical mass, they were displaced by Japanese laborers.

Japanese migrant laborers were accorded a similar reception. Before 1906, the *Mercury,* our barometer for the attitudes of the dominant class in the valley, was decidedly in favor of the Japanese presence. After 1906, however, when the Japanese began to dominate the valley's agricultural work force, the *Mercury's* editorials and news columns veered away from that position and joined in the call for Japanese exclusion. The newpaper's about-face reflected the increasing complexity of the anti-Japanese movement. Progressive politics sought Japanese dependence rather than expulsion because of the pragmatic gains reaped from that relationship. Public opinion and the alien land laws, thus did not drive the Japanese from the county or

from agriculture, but kept them in segregated communities, restricted their economic latitudes, and stunted their full development. Further, the dominant class divided the working class by aligning itself with white labor (the American Federation of Labor) on the basis of race, attacking the Japanese community as unassimilable and undesirable. Thus, the progressives were able to attain the homogeneity they sought for the valley's mainstream through segregation and the dual economy, while maintaining class privilege and profiting from the dependent Japanese farming community.

While the dominant class mapped out the terrain of oppression, the Japanese farmers altered the landscape through resistance. The infusion of women and their labor following 1907 made farm tenancy possible, and resulted in the establishment of permanent communities — farm clusters — in contrast to the bachelor society in Nihonmachi. Households maximized their incomes through full employment — including children and the aged — and through supplementary wage labor during the winter months. Japanese farmers survived and in some cases prospered by diversifying their crops, by utilizing the quick-growing but labor-intensive berries for start-ups, and by modifying and inventing farm machinery and techniques to meet their special needs. Their communities, the farming clusters, reinforced ethnic solidarity through the sharing of labor, tools, and wells; through social events such as picnics and New Year's Day celebrations; and through the Japanese language schools. Finally, Japanese cooperatives assisted in the marketing of crops, in reducing the costs of fertilizers, and other support functions.

The displacement of Japanese farmers during World War II was both opportune and consonant with the pattern of oppression and resistance. Like the anti-Chinese fervor of the 1870s and 1880s and the anti-Japanese movement around 1906, the mass removal of Japanese farmers from the valley in 1942 came at a critical time. Despite the constraints of dependency, Japanese farmers were making significant progress toward landownership. They supplied most of the vegetables for the local canneries, had expanded their markets to the East Coast, and were becoming more firmly entrenched in the valley's political economy. Their mass removal, thus, stymied the anticipated economic take-off of Japanese farmers in the valley. The white majority's concern over the expulsion of Japanese farmers was not motivated by humanitarianism but by economic self-interest. Once a solution had been reached for transferring those farms to non-Japanese operators, their initial reservations disappeared and exclusionist resolutions were passed by Morgan Hill, San Jose, and the county as a whole.

The return of Japanese farmers to the status of migrant laborers was most satisfactory to the valley's dominant class for at least two reasons. First, the returning Japanese provided essential agricultural labor, saved the fall harvest, and cultivated vast acreages of the extremely profitable strawberries. Second, the Japanese no longer posed a threat to the dominance of whites in agriculture. In fact, apart from the remaining orchards and fields, the Japanese were rapidly becoming irrelevant to the valley's diversified political economy. They were thus largely innocuous.

Although oppression cannot be denied, resistance and the persistence of the human spirit cannot forever be repulsed. We would like to end this testament to the tenacity of Japanese farmers in the Santa Clara Valley with an example of courage, humanism, and a reminder of what could be. Before the government announced the closing of the concentration camps, a group of black and white women undertook a study of the San Jose Nihonmachi area in anticipation of the return of Japanese Americans to the valley. Prominent among the women active in the rebuilding of the community were Anne Peabody, Marjorie Pitman, Evelyn Settles, and Nina Wolters. These women, along with members of the Council for Civic Unity of San Jose, took hot food to the arriving Japanese Americans and transported them from the train station to their places of lodging.[2] That reception was not unlike the scene at the San Jose Southern Pacific station three years earlier when white women handed out fruit, milk, and coffee to the departing Japanese. Perhaps the women recognized their common bond of oppression with the expelled and confined Japanese Americans; perhaps they were stirred by a profound sense of injustice. In any event, their simple act is an example of genuine fortitude and benevolence, and should be remembered.

The Council for Civic Unity and members of the Japanese American community — including Hisajiro Inouye, Torahiko Kawakami, Kohei Kogura, Shigio Masunaga, James Maruyama, Kunisaku Mineta, Kichitaro Okagaki, Eiichi Sakauye, and Harry Taketa — arranged and managed hostels for the homeless returning Japanese in San Jose.[3] Frank Sakata of Watsonville, owner of the Gilroy Hot Springs Resort, donated it for use as a hostel.[4] The various hostels in the county ultimately served nearly 2,000 returning Japanese Americans. Evelyn Settles, the last chairperson of the Hostel Committee of the Council for Civic Unity, summed up the work of the group in her final report dated June 12, 1946:

> So ends the work of a committee set up by the Civic Unity Council of San Jose 18 months ago. Many problems were met and solved that had not been dreamed of in those first months. There are many things that I am sure every member wished could have been done better, but each did the best he or she could under the circumstances. It has been a good year, for the friendships made have been real and are the kind that will endure. I wish that I could personally thank every committee member, and every one of the many friends who did so much to aid us, and could tell you of the splendid things each one did. . . . It is hoped that it [the report] gives some indication of the tremendous amount of effort which has been put into the enormous task of rehabilitating the thousands of worthy citizens who were so rudely displaced.[5]

The work of the Hostel Committee offers a model worthy of emulation. The restoration of the Japanese American community was at once collective and reciprocal.

The historical experience of Japanese farmers in the Santa Clara Valley exemplifies the contradictions inherent to capitalism. While oppressed, they resisted. They were united in a common ethnicity, and divided by class interests, of "bosses" and workers, large growers and tenant farmers. Their reaction to oppression was heroic and efficacious, anti-social and destructive. They were an integral and indispensible element in the valley's political economy, and isolated from and castigated by the wielders of power. They were manipulated by the dominant class, but they helped to shape their own history. That struggle is the Japanese legacy.

Footnotes

[1] Chiu, *Chinese Labor,* 82; and Chan, "Chinese in California Agriculture," 42.

[2] Girdner and Loftis, *Great Betrayal,* 408-09.

[3] Wayne Kanemoto, "The Return to San Jose," chapter included in the final report of the San Jose Commission on the Internment of Local Japanese Americans entitled, ". . .With Liberty and Justice For All," February 1985.

[4] *San Jose Mercury Herald,* September 9, 1945.

[5] Quoted in Kanemoto, "The Return."

Kakitsubata
IRIS

SELECT BIBLIOGRAPHY

ORAL HISTORIES

Akizuki, Masao, November 23, 1983; November 30, 1983; December 7, 1983.

Ando, Yoshio, October 26, 1983; November 2, 1983; November 11, 1983; January 19, 1984.

Araki, Harry, March 13, 1984; March 20, 1984.

Ezaki, Tom, January 27, 1984; February 2, 1984.

Filice, Michael J., Sr., February 14, 1984.

Hayakawa, John Y., February 24, 1984; March 2, 1984; March 8, 1984; March 15, 1984.

Inouye, Kaoru, August 22, 1984.

Kawahara, Katsusaburo, January 25, 1984; February 8, 1984.

Kawashima, Satoru, January 12, 1984; January 19, 1984.

Kurasaki, Henry, February 23, 1984.

Masunaga, Shigio, June 15, 1984; July 13, 1984.

Matsumura, Phil Y., February 16, 1984; February 23, 1984.

Matsumura, Sue (Sumiko), February 23, 1984.

Nakamura, Kazuto, March 13, 1984.

Omori, Hisao, November 2, 1983; November 9, 1983; November 15, 1983.

Sakauye, Eiichi, April 27, 1983; May 4, 1983.

Takeda, Shoji, December 21, 1983; December 29, 1983.

Tomita, Tad, March 16, 1984; March 23, 1984.

GOVERNMENT DOCUMENTS AND PUBLICATIONS

Bureau of the Census, Twelfth Census of the U.S. (1900), *Agriculture,* V, No. 1, Government Printing Office: Washington, D.C., 1902.

Bureau of the Census, Thirteenth Census of the U.S. (1910), *Agriculture, 1909 and 1910,* VI, Government Printing Office: Washington, D.C., 1913.

Bureau of the Census, Fourteenth Census of the U.S. (1920), *Agriculture,* VI, Government Printing Office: Washington, D.C., 1922.

Bureau of the Census, *U.S. Census of Agriculture: 1935,* I, Government Printing Office: Washington, D.C., 1936.

Bureau of the Census, *U.S. Census of Agriculture: 1945,* I, No. 30, Government Printing Office: Washington, D.C., 1946.

Bureau of the Census, *U.S. Census of Agriculture: 1954,* I, No. 33, Government Printing Office: Washington, D.C., 1956.

Divorce Cases, 1900-1953, Santa Clara County Superior Court.

Final Report, San Jose Commission on the Internment of Local Japanese Americans, February 1985.

Grantee/Grantor Files, 1910-1950, County Recorder's Office, Santa Clara County.

U.S. Congress, House Committee on Immigration and Naturalization, *Hearings,* 66th Congress, 2d Session, Government Printing Office: Washington, D.C., 1921.

U.S. Congress, House Select Committee, *National Defense Migration,* 77th Congress, 2d Session, Government Printing Office: Washington, D.C., 1942.

U.S. Congress, Senate, *Reports of the Immigration Commission,* XXIII, 61st Congress, 2d Session, Government Printing Office: Washington, D.C., 1911.

U.S. Congress, Senate, *Reports of the Immigration Commission,* XXIV, 61st Congress, 2d Session, Government Printing Office: Washington, D.C., 1911.

U.S. Congress, Senate, *Reports of the Immigration Commission,* I, 61st Congress, 3rd Session, Government Printing Office: Washington, D.C., 1911.

War Relocation Authority, *Evacuee Property Program of WRA, Northern Farms, Inc.*

War Relocation Authority, *People in Motion,* Government Printing Office: Washington, D.C., 1947.

War Relocation Authority, *Post-War Returns Statistics by County.*

War Relocation Authority, *Report of Activities of the Evacuee Property Program, July 1942-December 1943, Subjects: Agricultural Property Cases and Farm Security Administration Program.*

War Relocation Authority, *Returns to the West Coast — City, Cumulative,* Document 1, January 1-June 1, 1945; Document 2, January 1-August 15, 1945; and *Final Report,* Document 2, Number 12, January 1, 1945-March 31, 1946.

War Relocation Authority, *The Wartime Handling of Evacuee Property,* Government Printing Office: Washington, D.C., 1946.

War Relocation Authority, *WRA: A Story of Human Conservation,* Government Printing Office: Washington, D.C., 1946.

Wartime Civil Control Administration, Statistical Section, *Bulletin No. 6,* April 11, 1942; *Bulletin No. 7,* April 13, 1942; and *Bulletin No. 10,* May 15, 1942.

MANUSCRIPTS, UNPUBLISHED DISSERTATIONS, THESES

Alston, A., "A Brief History of the Fruit and Vegetable Industry of the Pacific Coast," manuscript, Simon J. Lubin Society, San Francisco, 1938.

Anthony, Donald, "Labor Conditions in the Canning Industry in Santa Clara Valley of the State of California," Ph.D. dissertation, Stanford University, 1928.

Arbuckle, Clyde, "San Jose's Governmental Seats Since 1777," manuscript, 1958.

"Articles of Incorporation and Bylaws," California Prune and Apricot Growers Association, San Jose, 1922.

Bray, George, "The Alviso Flouring Mills," manuscript, San Jose Historical Museum, 1920.

Cameron, Kenneth, "Association Bargaining in the California Canning Industry," M.A. thesis, University of California, Berkeley, 1949.

Chan, Sucheng, "Methodological Problems in the Study of Japanese Immigrant Activities in California Agriculture," paper delivered at the Ethnic Studies Symposium, University of California, Berkeley, November 30, 1978.

Cox, LaWanda, "Agricultural Labor in the United States, 1865-1900," Ph.D. dissertation, University of California, Berkeley, 1941.

Cummings, Scott Brian, "The Effect of Urban and Industrial Growth on the Social Backgrounds of Elected Public Officials," M.A. thesis, San Jose State University, 1968.

Fowler, Ruth, "Some Aspects of Public Opinion Concerning the Japanese in Santa Clara County," M.A. thesis, Stanford University, 1934.

Hirabayashi, Patti Jo N., "San Jose Nihonmachi," Master of Urban Planning thesis, San Jose State University, 1977.

Howell, Marjorie, "California Cannery Unions," M.A. thesis, Stanford University, 1946.

Ichihashi, Y., "Supplementary Report on the Japanese in the Watsonville District," Yamato Ichihashi Papers, Stanford University Archives, SC 71, Box 2, Folder 2.

Jamieson, Stuart Marshall, "Labor Unionism in Agriculture," Ph.D. dissertation, University of California, Berkeley, 1943.

Kai, Gunki, "Economic Status of the Japanese in California," M.A. thesis, Stanford University, 1920.

Laffey, Glory Anne, "The Chinatowns of San Jose," manuscript, 1979.

-----, "Water Management and Urban Growth in San Jose," M.A. thesis, 1982.

Mandich, Mitchell, "The Growth and Development of San Jose, California: Social Political and Economic Considerations," M.A. thesis, San Jose State University, 1975.

Martin, Richard G., "Water Conservation in the Santa Clara Valley," M.A. thesis, University of California, Berkeley, 1949.

Matsui, Shichiro, "Economic Aspects of the Japanese Situation in California," Ph.D. dissertation, University of California, Berkeley, 1922.

Matthews, Glenna, "A California Middletown. The Social History of San Jose in the Depression," Ph.D. dissertation, Stanford University, 1976.

Mortenson, F.N., "A Field Survey of the Need for a Farm Security Administration Camp for Migratory Agricultural Workers in Santa Clara County," Federal Archives and Records Center, San Bruno, CA, Farm Security Administration, Record Group 96, Box 42, File RR-CF 39, 201.

Nettler, Gwynne, "The Relationship Between Attitude and Information Concerning the Japanese in America," Ph.D. dissertation, Stanford University, 1945.

Palmer, Hans C., "Italian Immigration and the Development of California Agriculture," Ph.D. dissertation, University of California, Berkeley, 1965.

Phillips, Peter W., "Toward An Historical Theory of Wage Structures: The Evolution of Wages in California Canneries, 1970 to the Present," Ph.D. dissertation, Stanford University, 1980.

Ray, Sharon, "Santa Clara County and the Alien Land Initiative of 1920," paper presented to the California Pioneers Society of Santa Clara County, 1963.

Reynolds, Charles, "Oriental-White Relations in Santa Clara County," Ph.D. dissertation, Stanford, 1927.

Riggio, Joseph, "A Study of the San Jose Mayfair Area," M.A. thesis, San Jose State University, 1967.

Ruiz, Vicki Lynn, "UCAPAWA, Chicanas, and the Food Processing Industry, 1937-1950," Ph.D. dissertation, Stanford University, 1982.

Schmitt, Dorothea Louise, "History of Santa Clara Valley: The American Period, 1946-1865," M.A. thesis, University of California, Berkeley, 1928.

Takeda, Shoji, "Autobiography and Biography," n.d.

Thorpe, Robert, "Council-Manager Government in San Jose, California," M.A. thesis, Stanford University, 1938.

Timms, Gracy E., "Santa Clara County: The Agrarian Past and the Challenge of the Future," M.A. thesis, San Jose State University, 1981.

Tognazzini, Wilma, "Pioneers in California," manuscript, San Jose Historical Museum Archives, n.d.

Vatter, Ethel Landau, "The California Canning Industry, 1910-1935: An Historical Survey," M.A. thesis, University of California, Berkeley, 1952.

Yagasaki, Noritaka, "Ethnic Cooperativism and Immigrant Culture: A Study of Japanese Floriculture and Truck Farming in California," Ph.D. dissertation, University of California, Berkeley, 1982.

Zambetti, Robert, "The Japanese in Santa Clara County, 1940-1950," paper presented to the Santa Clara County Pioneers Association, 1967.

BOOKS

Alesch, Daniel J. and Robert A. Levine, *Growth in San Jose,* Rand Corporation: Santa Monica, CA, 1973.

Arguments Against the California Alien Land Law, American Committee of Justice: Oakland, CA, 1920.

Barrett, Dick, ed., *A Century of Service: San Jose's 100 Year Old Business Firms,* n.p., n.d.

Beilharz, Edwin A. and Donald O. DeMers, *San Jose: California's First City,* Continental Heritage Press: Tulsa, 1980.

Bloom, Leonard and Ruth Reimer, *Removal and Return,* University of California Press: Berkeley, CA. 1949.

Bonacich, Edna, *The Economic Basis of Ethnic Solidarity: Small Business in the Japanese American Community,* University of California Press: Berkeley, CA., 1980.

Braznell, William, *California's Finest: The History of Del Monte Corporation and the Del Monte Brand,* Del Monte Corporation: San Francisco, 1982.

Broek, Jan Otto Marius, *The Santa Clara Valley, California: A Study in Landscape Changes,* N.V.A. Oosthoek's Uitgevers-Mij: Utrecht, 1932.

Brown, Alice M., *Japanese in Florin,* n.p., n.d.

Bunje, Emil T.H. *The Story of Japanese Farming in California,* University of California, Berkeley, 1937.

Butler, Phyllis Filiberti, *The Valley of Santa Clara,* Presidio Press, Novato, CA., 1975.

California Pioneers of Santa Clara County, Santa Clara County Pioneer Papers, Smith and McKay Printing: San Jose, 1973.

Chambers, Clarke A., *California Farm Organizations: A Historical Study of the Grange, the Farm Bureau and the Associated Farmers, 1929-1941,* University of California Press: Berkeley, 1952.

Cheng, Lucie and Edna Bonacich, eds., *Labor Immigration Under Capitalism: Asian Workers in the United States Before World War II,* University of California Press: Berkeley, 1984.

Chiu, Ping, *Chinese Labor in California: An Economic Study,* State Historical Society of Wisconsin: Madison, 1967.

Chuman, Frank, *The Bamboo People: The Law and Japanese Americans,* Publishers, Inc.: Del Mar, CA, 1976.

Cinel, Dino, *From Italy to San Francisco: The Immigrant Experience,* Stanford University Press: Stanford, 1982.

Commercial History of San Jose, California, Metropolitan Publishing Co.: San Jose, 1892.

Couchman, Robert, *The Sunsweet Story,* Sunsweet Growers: San Jose, 1967.

Cozzens, George, *Nine Men and 100 Years of Water History,* San Jose Water Works: San Jose, 1967.

Cunningham, Florence, *Saratoga's First Hundred Years,* Harlan Young Press: San Jose, 1967.

Daniel, Cletus, *Bitter Harvest: A History of California Farm Workers: 1870-1941,* University of California Press: Berkeley, 1981.

Daniels, Roger, *The Politics of Prejudice: The Anti-Japanese Movement in California and the Struggle for Japanese Exclusion,* University of California Press: Berkeley, 1962.

Eakins, David W., ed., *Businessmen and Municipal Reform: A Study of Ideals and Practice in San Jose and Santa Cruz, 1896-1916,* Sourisseau Academy for California State and Local History, San Jose State University: San Jose, 1976.

Foote, H.S., ed., *Pen Pictures From the Garden of the World,* The Lewis Publishing Company: Chicago, 1888.

Fox, Frances, *Bibliography: Santa Clara Valley Books and Booklets,* San Jose Historical Museum: San Jose, n.d.

Frish, John Powell, *Japanese Farmers in California,* n.p.: Oakland, 1919 (?).

Fukuda, Moritoshi, *Legal Problems of Japanese-Americans,* Keio Tsushin Co., Ltd.: Tokyo, 1980.

Girdner, Audrie and Anne Loftis, *The Great Betrayal: The Evacuation of the Japanese-Americans During World War II,* Macmillan Company: London, 1969.

Hall, Frederic, *The History of San Jose,* A.L. Bancroft and Co.: San Francisco, 1871.

Hermann, F.C. and G.A. Elliot, *Report on the Appraisement of Property of the San Jose Water Company,* Rincon Publishing Co.: San Francisco, 1913.

Historical Atlas Map of Santa Clara County, Thompson and West: San Francisco, 1876.

Hokubei Mainichi Yearbook, 1950.

Hom, Gloria Sun, ed., *Chinese Argonauts: An Anthology of the Chinese Contributions to the Historical Development of Santa Clara County,* California History Center, Foothill Junior College: Los Altos Hills, CA, 1971.

Horsman, Reginald, *Race and Manifest Destiny: The Origins of American Racial Anglo-Saxonism,* Harvard University Press: Cambridge, MA, 1981.

Hosokawa, Bill, *Nisei: The Quiet Americans,* William Morrow & Co.: New York, 1969.

Howard, Fred K., *History of Sun Maid Growers,* Sun Maid Raisin Growers: n.p., 1922.

Humphrey, Janet, *From Blossoms to the World,* Foothill Joint Junior College District: Cupertino, CA, 1970.

Ichihashi, Yamato, *Japanese Immigration,* Japanese Association of America: San Francisco, 1913.

-----, *Japanese in the United States,* Arno Press: New York, 1969.

Irons, Peter, *Justice At War,* Oxford University Press: New York, 1983.

Iyenaga, T. and Kenoske Sato, *Japan and the California Problem,* G.P. Putnam's Sons: New York, 1921.

James, Marquis and Bessie Rowland, *Biography of a Bank: The Story of Bank of America,* Harper and Brothers: New York, 1954.

James, William amd George McMurray, *History of San Jose,* G.H. McMurray: San Jose, 1933.

The Japanese in California: Comments in the California Press, n.p.: n.p., 1920.

The Japanese Farmers in California, The Japanese Agricultural Association: San Francisco, 1918.

Jelinek, Lawrence J., *Harvest Empire: A History of California Agriculture,* Boyd and Fraser: San Francisco, 1979.

Johnsen, Julia E., comp., *Japanese Exclusion,* The H.W. Wilson Co.: New York, 1925.

Johnson, Hiram, *Anti-Alien Legislation in California,* n.p.: San Jose, 1913.

Kawakami, K.K., *The Real Japanese Question,* MacMillan and Co.: New York, 1921.

Kessler, James and Kan Ori, *Anti-Japanese Land Law Controversy in California: A Case Study of International and Intranational Communications as Affected by the Dynamics of American Federalism,* Sophia University: Tokyo, 1968.

Kraemer, Erich and H.E. Erdman, *History of Cooperation in the Marketing of California Fresh Deciduous Fruits,* University of California Agricultural Experiment Station: Berkeley, 1933.

Leung, Peter C.Y., *One Day, One Dollar: Locke, California and the Chinese Farming Experience in the Sacramento Delta,* Chinese/Chinese American History Project: El Cerrito, CA, 1984.

McClatchy, V.S., *Japanese Immigration and Colonization,* R and E Research Associates: San Francisco, 1970.

McCurdy, Rahno Mobel, *The History of the California Fruit Growers Exchange,* G. Rice and Sons: Los Angeles, 1925.

McWilliams, Carey, *Brothers Under the Skin,* Little, Brown and Company: Boston, 1964.

-----, *Factories in the Field,* Peregrine Publishers, Inc.: Santa Barbara, 1971.

-----, *Prejudice: Japanese Americans, Symbol of Racial Intolerance,* Archon Books: Hamden, Connecticut, 1971.

Majka, Linda and Theo, *Farmworkers, Agribusiness and the State,* Temple University Press: Philadelphia, 1982.

Mann, Arthur, ed., *The Progressive Era: Liberal Rennaissance or Liberal Failure,* Holt, Rinehart and Winston: New York, 1963.

Mears, Elliot G., *Resident Orientals on the American Pacific Coast,* Institute of Pacific Relations: New York, 1927.

Miller, Stuart Creighton, *The Unwelcome Immigrant: The American Image of the Chinese, 1785-1882,* University of California Press: Berkeley, 1969.

Millis, H.A., *The Japanese Problem in the United States,* The MacMillan Co.: New York, 1920.

Misawa, Steven, ed., *Beginnings: Japanese Americans in San Jose,* Japanese American Community Senior Service: San Jose, 1981.

Modell, John, *The Economics and Politics of Racial Accomodation: The Japanese of Los Angeles,* University of Illinois Press: Urbana, 1977.

Munro-Fraser, J.P., *The History of Santa Clara County,* Alley, Bowen and Co.: San Francisco, 1881.

Myer, Dillon S., *Uprooted Americans,* University of Arizona Press, Tucson, 1971.

Naka, Kaizo, *Social and Economic Conditions Among Japanese Farmers in California,* R and E Research Associates: San Francisco, 1974.

Naturipe Berry Growers, San Jose, 1977.

The Naturipe Story, n.p., n.d.

New World Sun Yearbook, 1940.

Pajus, Jean, *The Real Japanese California,* James H. Gillick: Berkeley, 1937.

Poli, Adon, *Japanese Farm Holdings on the Pacific Coast,* University of California, Davis College of Agriculture: Davis, CA, 1944.

Rice, Bertha, *The Builders of Our Valley,* n.p.: San Jose, 1957.

Rogin, Michael and John Shover, *Political Change in California,* Greenwood Press: Westport, CT, 1970.

Salmon, David W., *The Metropolitan Area of Santa Clara County, California,* Stanford University Press: Stanford, 1946.

Sandmeyer, Elmer, *The Anti-Chinese Movement in California,* University of Illinois Press: Chicago, 1973.

San Jose Chamber of Commerce, *Santa Clara County, California,* Wright and Eley Co.: San Jose, 1924.

San Jose City Directories.

Sarasohn, Eileen Sunada, ed., *The Issei: Portrait of A Pioneer,* Pacific Books: Palo Alto, CA, 1983.

Sawyer, Eugene, *History of Santa Clara County, California,* Historic Record Co.: Los Angeles, 1922.

Saxton, Alexander, *The Indispensable Enemy: Labor and the Anti-Chinese Movement in California,* University of California Press: Berkeley, 1971.

Shaw, Frederic, et al., *Oil Lamps and Iron Ponies,* El Camino Press: Salinas, CA, 1949.

Shima, George, *An Appeal to Justice: The Injustice of the Proposed Initiative Measure,* Farmers and Merchants Bank Building: Stockton, n.d.

Starr, Kevin, *Americans and the California Dream,* Oxford University Press: New York, 1973.

Strong, Edward K., *Japanese in California,* Stanford University Press: Stanford, 1933.

Sunshine, Fruit and Flowers: Santa Clara County and Its Resources, San Jose Mercury Publishing Co.: San Jose, 1895.

Walsh, James P., *The San Francisco Irish: 1850-1976,* Smith McKay Printing Co.: San Jose, 1978.

Wickson, E.J., *Rural California,* Rural, State and Province Series: New York, 1923.

ARTICLES

Bailey, Thomas A., "California, Japan and the Alien Land Legislation of 1913," *Pacific Historical Review,* 1:1 (March 1932), 36-59.

Borchers, Irma, "Legislation Against the Oriental Farmer," *Journal of Land and Public Utility Economics,* 1:4 (October 1925), 509-512.

Chan, Sucheng, "Using Califonia Archives for Research in Chinese American History," *Annals of the Chinese Historical Society of the Pacific Northwest,* Seattle, 1983.

Eliot, Albert and Guy Calden, "The Law Affecting Japanese Residing in the State of California," in Roger Daniels, ed., *Three Short Works on Japanese Americans,* Arno Press: New York, 1978.

Ferguson, Edwin E., "The California Alien Land Law and the 14th Amendment," *California Law Review,* 35 (1947), 61-90.

Fugita, Stephen S. and David O'Brien, "Economics, Ideology and Ethnicity: The Struggle Between the United Farm Workers and the Nisei Farmers League," *Social Problems,* 25:2 (December 1977), 146-156.

Higgs, Robert, "Landless by Law: the Japanese Immigrants in California Agriculture to 1941," *Journal of Economic History,* 38:1 (March 1978): 205-225.

-----, "The Wealth of Japanese Tenant Farmers in California, 1909," *Agricultural History,* 53:1 (January 1979), 488-493.

Hoffman, Abraham, "The El Monte Berry Picker's Strike, 1933," *Journal of the West,* 12:1 (January 1973), 71-84.

Iwata, Masakazu, "Japanese Immigrants in California Agriculture," *Agricultural History,* 36:1 (January 1962), 25-37.

Keroher, Grace Cable, "California's Anti-Orientalism," in Clarence Peters, comp., *The Immigration Problem,* H.W. Wilson Co.: New York, 1948, 178-86.

Kido, Saburo, "The Alien Land Law," *The Berkeley Lyceum* (publication of the Japanese Students' Club of the University of California, Berkeley), April 1926, 19-22.

Lopez, Ronald W., "The El Monte Berry Strike of 1933," *Aztlán,* 1:1 (Spring 1970), 101-115.

McWilliams, Carey, "Moving the West Coast Japanese," *Harper's Magazine,* 185:1108 (September 1942).

-----, "Once Again the 'Yellow Peril'," *The Nation,* 140:3651 (June 26, 1935).

McGovney, Dudley O., "The Anti-Japanese Land Laws of California and Ten Other States," *California Law Review,* 35 (1947), 7-60.

Modell, John, "Class or Ethnic Solidarity: The Japanese American Company Union," *Pacific Historical Review,* 38:2 (May 1969), 193-206.

Okihiro, Gary Y. (with) David Drummond, "The Concentration Camps and Japanese Economic Losses in California Agriculture, 1900-1942," in Sandra C. Taylor, Harry Kitano, and Roger Daniels, eds., *From Relocation to Redress: Japanese Americans, 1942-1983,* University of Utah Press: Salt Lake City, 1985.

Poli, Adon and Warren Engstrand, "Japanese Agriculture on the Pacific Coast," *Journal of Land and Public Utility Economics,* 2:4 (November 1945), 352-364.

Reid, Joseph D., Jr., "Sharecropping in History and Theory," *Agricultural History,* 49:2 (April 1975), 426-440.

Saloutos, Theodore, "The Immigrant in Pacific Coast Agriculture, 1880-1940," *Agricultural History,* 49:1 (January 1975), 182-201.

Spaulding, Charles, "The Mexican Strike at El Monte, California," *Sociology and Social Research,* 18:6 (July-August 1934), 571-580.

"Tad Tomita: Strawberry Success Story," *Western Grower & Shipper,* 49:9 (September 1978), 6-7, 9.

Taylor, Frank J., "Home Again," *Collier's,* February 15, 1947, 15, 34-36.

Taylor, Paul S. and Tom Vasey, "Historical Background of California Farm Labor," *Rural Sociology,* 1:3 (September 1936), 289-295.

Wollenberg, Charles, "Race and Class in California: "The El Monte Berry Strike of 1933," California *Historical Quarterly,* 51:2 (Summer 1972), 155-164.

INDEX

Colophon

Book production by Seonaid McArthur
Index by Malyndia D. Sellers
Cover and jacket design by Dan DiVittorio
Text design by Roy Hirabayashi
Composed in CG Bem
by Communicart, Santa Clara, California
Cover printed on Simpson Gainsborough
Text printed on Mead Offset Enamel
by Edwards Brothers, Ann Arbor, Michigan